The Posture
POSITIONED FOR THE PROPHETIC

LOVY ELIAS

Copyright © 2025 Lovy L. Elias

All rights reserved. The total or partial reproduction of this book is forbidden under any of its forms, neither graphic, electronic or audiovisual, without previous written authorization from publishers.

ISBN:
978-1-7374067-0-9 Hardcover
978-1-7374067-1-6 eBook

Unless otherwise specified, Bible verses are taken from the King James Version (KJV), and the Hebrew and Greek word references are from James Strong's *Exhaustive Concordance of the Bible*, originally published in 1980.

Published by:
Prophet Lovy Ministries in collaboration with Petran Publishing.

Made and printed in the USA.

To my father and mother,
Lovy Mokolo and Mado Zaina Longomba,
who are with the Lord.
To my uncle, Reverend Simon Ngizulu,
who is my foundation in Christ.
To all the fathers and mentors
who have brought me up to this point.
To the Church of Jesus Christ,
the only begotten Son of God.
Grace and peace to us all.

CONTENTS

FOREWORD		v
INTRODUCTION		1
One	FINDING THE VOICE OF GOD	9
Two	DESIRING THE PROPHETIC	23
Three	PURITY OF THE SOUL	35
Four	THE SIN THAT SILENCES GOD	57
Five	PROPHETIC PRAYERS	69
Six	PROPHETS FROM THE WOMB	85
Seven	IMPARTATION AND MENTORSHIP	95
Eight	THE LAWS OF IMPARTATION	101
Nine	MYSTERIES AND SECRETS	113
Ten	PROPHETIC CONSCIOUSNESS	129
Eleven	MASTERING THE FLOW OF THE SPIRIT	137
Twelve	SERVING ANOTHER'S VISION	177
Thirteen	DEFILED VESSELS	189
Fourteen	PROPHETIC DEPTH	201
Fifteen	FEAR IN THE PROPHETIC	209
Sixteen	GOD'S LANGUAGE	219
Conclusion	HE THAT HATH AN EAR	269

FOREWORD

Paul Tillich said, "Revelation must be given, and revelation must be received, or it is not revelation." He expands on this thought prolifically by saying, "Theology moves back and forth between two poles, the eternal truth of its foundation and the temporal situation in which the eternal truth must be received." Not "unless it is received." Again, revelation's reality depends on its reception.

The substratum of the prophetic is Paul Tillich's "temporal situation in which the eternal truth must be received." Therefore, it is a direct answer from an eternal scriptural truth for a present dilemma, or a destiny assignment.

Lovy's declaration of eternal scriptural truth is consistently visible in his revelation for the temporal situation. His prophetic is grounded in the profundity of God's eternal word, because only God can extrapolate immediate remedies from His colossal library of eternal truth and reveal them to His Prophet to surgically solve complex problems.

Accuracy in the prophetic is paramount. Habakkuk declares, "Write the vision, and make it plain upon the tablets, that he may run that reads it." The chaos caused by inaccuracy in the prophetic would be cataclysmic for continued faith and love for a word from the Lord. Not only would the reader not know when to run, where to run, how to run, or stand still, but the prophet's revelatory accuracy is the difference between truth and fiction, chaos and destiny, life and death.

The writer's intensity for accuracy is a constructive collaboration for the need to teach those who are inclined or are called to the prophetic ministry. Upon reading this work, you will know whether you have a legitimate call from God or not. Lovy intends to mature the individuals called of God and separate them from those who have no business in the prophetic.

Immediately after the opening chapter, Lovy informs the reader that the purity of the soul is essential for revelatory experiences, and there is a sin that silences God. The prophet void of character is without a word from the Lord, which nullifies "revelation must be given and must be received." There is no prophecy if revelation is not given.

Early in his writings, the writer shows that the prophet's character can obfuscate his revelatory experience. He proves that revelation for the prophetic is connected directly to a relationship with the Supreme Revelator. Where character declines, revelation for the prophetic becomes an indiscernible whisper. The raucous noise of the flesh drowns out the voice of God in the prophet's spirit.

To the pure in soul, Lovy plunges headlong into every aspect of grasping and understanding the prophetic. He is teaching, informing, instructing, and inspiring his readers. He is not only deeply theological, but his personal struggles, failures, and successes are transparently expressed to ensure relatability to his readers. He is holding nothing back to jettison every prophet to maturity.

I am particularly enamored by the chapter "Serving Another's Vision." This chapter puts the book and its information at every Christian's disposal, whether we have a prophetic anointing or not. What better way to enhance your calling to serve any prophet's vision, than having an extensive understanding of the prophetic anointing that this work reveals?

Lovy's genuine love for the truth involved in the revelatory experience endorses Sister Julie B. Beck's words, "The ability to qualify for, receive, and act on personal revelation is the single most important skill that can be acquired in this life."

Obviously, this book's writer, Lovy Elias, wants you to stir your gift and express "the most important skill that can be acquired in this life." The Posture is a must-read!

Bishop Noel Jones
Senior Pastor
City of Refuge

INTRODUCTION

For generations, believers have been robbed of their inheritance through doctrines that silence the voice of God. Many have been taught that He no longer speaks, except through the Bible. They are told that revelation ceased with the Apostles, and that divine encounters are for an elite few. These teachings are not only misleading, they are unbiblical. The Scriptures themselves testify that the Word is not a manuscript but a Person.

> *"In the beginning was the Word, and the Word was with God, and the Word was God."*
> John 1:1

If Jesus is alive, then He still speaks. To say otherwise is to strip Him of His living nature and reduce Him to history.

Those who gave us the Scriptures did not begin with a book; they began with a voice. Moses heard Him on Sinai. The Prophets of old saw visions and received instructions directly from His mouth. The Apostles walked with Christ, and even after His ascension, His Spirit spoke to them, guided them, and revealed mysteries. To confine God to text alone is to deny the very experiences of those who penned the text.

I was grieved by this error from an early age. As a child, God appeared to me, not because I prayed for it, but because He chose me. His voice introduced His Person to me long before I could study or debate theology. That encounter became my compass, and from that moment on, I could never accept the lie that God is mute. Yet, as I grew older, I discovered that many who taught about God spoke of a God they had studied but never met. They were trained in classrooms, but not in His presence. As a result, they could only repeat doctrines they had learned without ever having truly heard from the Living Word Himself.

Oftentimes, I noticed that the "voice of the Lord" was invoked only when it was time to raise an offering. Outside of that, His voice was absent from their ministries. As a young boy who heard God daily, I was left wondering, *Which Lord are we speaking of?* Because the One I knew did not appear only when money was involved.

These wrong teachings delay destinies, confuse believers, and leave many powerless. I have seen lives stagnate simply because they were never taught that God wanted to speak to them personally. Their delays were not even their own fault; they were simply the fruit of what they had been taught.

From the beginning of my journey, I knew God had sent me to be a disruptor; that He sent me to confront error and to shake systems that had grown comfortable yet void of His presence. The goal of this book is for you to realize that God *wants* to talk to you, and He is already speaking. "The Posture" is the key, the missing link. These pages carry both urgency and invitation: urgency to shake off what has delayed you, and an invitation to step into the alignment that causes His voice to become clear. This book is born from a burden to correct misinformation and reveal the posture that positions you to hear God clearly. My prayer is that as you read, every blockage will be removed and you will be rightly positioned to hear His voice.

INTRODUCTION

WHAT IS POSTURE

Posture is simply positioning. Posture is alignment. Just as the body must be rightly positioned to carry weight or perform with strength, the spirit must be rightly positioned to receive from God. If an athlete enters the gym with poor form, his effort will not only fail to produce results; it may cause injury. In the same way, if a believer approaches the things of the Spirit with pride, ignorance, or ambition, his pursuit will end in frustration.

Posture is the state of your heart, mind, and spirit before God. It is humility before Him, reverence toward Him, dependence upon Him, surrender to Him, and readiness to receive correction and instruction from Him. Without the right posture, every pursuit becomes vain.

GOD'S VOICE

The Hebrew word for voice is *qol* (קוֹל). It is not merely sound; it is vibration, resonance, and thunder. In Psalm 29, the voice of the Lord is described as shaking the wilderness, splitting the cedars, and making creation tremble. This is not a soft suggestion. When God speaks, the atmosphere responds. His voice carries creative weight. It does not just inform; it transforms. The Greek word *phōnē* (φωνή) adds another layer. Though it means sound or utterance, it also means a call or a summons. The voice of God is not just something you hear; it is something that draws you and pulls you into alignment, into obedience, and into destiny.

God's voice is constant; His *qol* is sounding right now. However, if your spirit is out of tune, His words will sound faint.

Apostle Paul warned us that without understanding *"the meaning of the voice,"* you become as a foreigner to the one speaking (1 Corinthians 14:11). Posture is what tunes your spirit to the right frequency so that what was once just background noise becomes a clear instruction. It is like adjusting a radio until the static disappears and the music comes alive. When you are rightly aligned, His *qol* becomes your guidance system, and His *phōnē* becomes your personal invitation to step into the next level of your assignment.

WHY POSTURE MATTERS

The Hebrew word for repentance is *shuv* (שׁוּב), which means to turn back, or to return to where you belong. It is not a word of punishment but of restoration. When God says, "Repent," He is not saying you should cry more or feel worse about yourself; He is rather saying, "Come home." To repent comes from the Greek word *metanoia* (μετάνοια), which goes even deeper. It literally means to change your mind, or to think differently. Repentance is not just about avoiding sin; it is about stepping back into alignment with heaven's reality. It is a re-calibration of your entire life to agree with what God is saying.

Many have been taught that repentance is groveling at the altar, beating yourself up, or trying to earn God's approval again. That is religion talking. True repentance is the opposite; it is the moment you stop running, turn toward Him, and say, "I agree with You." The moment you do, His voice becomes clear again. Repentance is not about paying for your mistakes; Jesus already did that. Repentance is about positioning yourself so that His words, His power, and His direction can flow without obstruction.

INTRODUCTION

Until you *shuv*, until you *metanoia*, you cannot hear Him accurately. The signal is blocked, not because God is far, but because you are facing the wrong direction. Repentance is simply turning the antenna of your spirit back toward heaven so you catch the broadcast again. The truth is that God is always speaking; the issue is our positioning. Mental clutter, emotional wounds, and spiritual immaturity are the postures that block the signal of heaven. Conversely, alignment, humility, and readiness are the postures that tune your spirit to hear.

Jesus confronted this same unawareness when He said,

"Ye do err, not knowing the scriptures, nor the power of God"
Matthew 22:29

Notice His rebuke: error comes not only from misinterpreting Scripture but from neglecting the power of God. Scripture and power are not rivals; they are companions. One records His voice; the other manifests it. To live by one without the other is to live half a life.

WHAT YOU WILL DISCOVER

My desire is not to mystify God further; rather, it is to demystify the prophetic life. This book was ordained by God for you in this very moment. It is not by chance that you are holding it. This is a predestined encounter, a divine appointment designed for you to know Him more deeply.

If you approach this book with the right posture, you will discover three realities:

1. **GOD IS NEARER THAN YOU THINK**
   His silence was never absence but an invitation to realign. He is not distant. He is approachable, and He longs to walk with you.

2. **THE PROPHETIC IS NOT ORNAMENTAL**
   It is the means by which God ushers His will, directs destinies, and saves souls. His voice is never for decoration; it is always for salvation.

3. **YOUR POSTURE DETERMINES YOUR RECEPTION**
   The gifts of God cannot be earned, but they can be missed. Alignment positions you to receive what ambition never will.

The prophetic is not reserved for a chosen few or "special" people. God introduces Himself to one for the benefit of many. Every prophetic voice becomes a contact point for the whole body. When one hears, all may hear.

AN INVITATION TO THE READER

Beloved, if you are holding this book, it is because God has ordained for you to draw nearer. Clear your mind of doctrines that told you He cannot speak. Lay aside the excuses of age or background. Whether you are fifteen or fifty, the prophetic is not out of reach. However, in order to receive, you must come empty. Forget what you think you know, because if what you knew was enough, you would already be walking in the fullness of His voice. Come like a child, ready to be taught, corrected, and filled afresh.

This book is not theory; it is preparation. If you grasp the

INTRODUCTION

essence of the pages before you, I assure you that you will hear God for yourself. As I often say, you cannot give what you do not have. I am qualified to teach you these things because, by God's mercy, I have been graced to walk this life in alignment with His voice. I can hear Him, and I can inquire of Him at any time. At times, I have even had to tone down my supernatural sensitivity simply to function normally, for I have mastered through discipline the posture of continually positioning myself to hear Yahweh. So, hear me by the Spirit of the Living God: I know what I am speaking of.

The prophetic is the instrument God uses to usher in His coming. If we cannot discern His voice, we cannot discern His times. And if we cannot discern His times, we cannot bring souls into His kingdom. This is the true end of prophecy: not spectacle, but salvation.

Prayer

Father, in the name of Jesus Christ, I pray for every reader of this book. Let the Spirit of wisdom, understanding, and revelation rest upon them. Reveal Yourself to them beyond what they have known.

Open their ears to hear You, open their eyes to see You, and open their hearts to receive You. Strip away every false teaching that has blinded them, and position them in humility to be filled.

Grant them grace beyond what You gave me, for the sake of their families, their nations, and for the salvation of souls. May they hear Your voice, carry it with integrity, and become vessels of the prophetic that prepare the earth for your coming.

Amen. Teleo.

One
FINDING THE VOICE OF GOD

ONE // FINDING THE VOICE OF GOD

THE CRY OF EVERY BELIEVER

> *"My sheep hear My voice, and I know them, and they follow Me."*
> John 10:27

One of the deepest cries I hear from believers across the world is, "Why can't I hear the voice of God?" This question is often asked in frustration. Some express how they used to hear Him clearly, but now they don't. Their dreams and visions have stopped, and even their intuition feels silent. While the voice of God is never absent, it resonates in specific locations within the human spirit. Unless a believer understands these locations and the divine order behind them, His voice will seem distant.

Beloved, the issue is not that God has stopped speaking. Understand that this silence is often an invitation; it presses you to ask deeper questions, to realign, to remember that God's voice is not random but always tied to His eternal purpose. If you grasp this revelation, your frustration will turn into clarity, and clarity into confidence.

LIFE IS PRIMARILY SPIRITUAL

Before we can understand how God speaks, we must first accept that life itself is primarily spiritual. Everything in the natural is a shadow of the eternal. Paul writes:

> *"For the things which are seen are temporal; but the things which are not seen are eternal."*
> 2 Corinthians 4:18

The physical world is not the foundation; it is the reflection. Every event you face, whether painful or joyous, or whether it feels like a victory or a failure, carries eternal significance. Even the struggles you endure are not empty; they are instruments shaping your alignment with destiny. This is why some fail to hear God's voice. They try to interpret life only through the natural, forgetting that the natural is only the echo of spiritual reality. Once you awaken to this truth, you realize that His voice is not lost, but has always been speaking from the place of purpose.

PURPOSE AND CALLING: WHERE THE VOICE BEGINS

Every human spirit sent by God into the world was sent with a divine purpose. No man or woman is accidental. Before that purpose is fully revealed, however, there is a stage known as calling.

- Purpose is God's complete intention for your life; it is the final destination He foresaw before you were even born.
- Calling is the divine summons that draws you toward that intention.

The very first time God's voice is heard in the soul of man is through conviction.

> *"And when He is come, He will reprove the world of sin, and of righteousness, and of judgment."*
> John 16:8

The Spirit convicts, awakens, and plants the seed of

ONE // FINDING THE VOICE OF GOD

salvation. That is the first echo of His voice.

The second echo comes on the journey into purpose. It is here that His instructions, corrections, and confirmations are heard most clearly. Anything outside of purpose feels like silence, not because He has stopped speaking, but because His voice does not operate outside of His eternal intention. Paul confirms this:

> *"Who hath saved us, and called us with an holy calling, not according to our works, but according to His own purpose and grace, which was given us in Christ Jesus before the world began."*
> 2 Timothy 1:9

Calling and purpose are the anchor points of the divine voice.

THE VOICE WITHIN PURPOSE

When you are aligned with purpose, even your failures cannot silence the voice of God. Look at David. He sinned grievously by murdering Uriah and taking Bathsheba, yet God did not abandon him. Instead, He extended His hand through the prophet Nathan, bringing correction and restoration. Even more profound is this: from that very union came Solomon, the wisest man to ever live.

God did not endorse David's sin, but He used even the brokenness to serve His eternal plan, because David was still within the borders of his purpose. This teaches us a crucial truth: the voice of God is not sustained by human perfection but by divine alignment. When you are in purpose, His voice will reach you even in correction.

THE VOICE THAT REDIRECTS FUNCTION INTO PURPOSE

The voice of God does not only convict and correct, it also redirects. God often meets His people in the place of their earthly function and reveals their eternal assignment.

- **PETER**

While casting his nets, the Lord Jesus called him.

> *"And Jesus, walking by the sea of Galilee, saw two brethren, Simon called Peter, and Andrew his brother, casting a net into the sea: for they were fishers. And He saith unto them, Follow Me, and I will make you fishers of men."*
> Matthew 4:19

His trade became the prophetic picture of his calling.

- **MOSES**

While tending Jethro's flock, he encountered the burning bush.

> *"Now Moses kept the flock of Jethro his father in law, the priest of Midian: and he led the flock to the backside of the desert, and came to the mountain of God, even to Horeb.*
> *And the angel of the LORD appeared unto him in a flame of fire out of the midst of a bush: and he looked, and, behold, the bush burned with fire, and the bush was not consumed.*
> *And Moses said, I will now turn aside, and see this great sight, why the bush is not burnt.*

ONE // FINDING THE VOICE OF GOD

> *And when the LORD saw that he turned aside to see, God called unto him out of the midst of the bush, and said, Moses, Moses. And he said, Here am I."*
> Exodus 3:1-4

Shepherding sheep was the preparation for shepherding Israel.

- **GIDEON**

While threshing wheat in fear, the Angel of the Lord appeared to him.

> *"And there came an angel of the LORD, and sat under an oak which was in Ophrah, that pertained unto Joash the Abiezrite: and his son Gideon threshed wheat by the winepress, to hide it from the Midianites.*
> *And the angel of the LORD appeared unto him, and said unto him, The LORD is with thee, thou mighty man of valour."*
> Judges 6:11-12

God's voice transformed his weakness into courage.

- **ELISHA**

While plowing with oxen, Elijah cast his cloak on him.

> *"So he departed thence, and found Elisha the son of Shaphat, who was plowing with twelve yoke of oxen before him, and he with the twelfth: and Elijah passed by him, and cast his mantle upon him."*
> 1 Kings 19:19

Faithful labor in the field positioned him for prophetic

succession.

- **AMOS**

    A herdsman and gatherer of sycamore fruit, yet God lifted him into the prophetic office.

    > *"Then answered Amos, and said to Amaziah, I was no prophet, neither was I a prophet's son; but I was an herdman, and a gatherer of sycomore fruit:*
    > *And the LORD took me as I followed the flock, and the LORD said unto me, Go, prophesy unto my people Israel."*
    > Amos 7:14-15

    His obscurity became his launching point.

- **DAVID**

    Found among the sheep when Samuel anointed him king.

    > *"And Samuel said unto Jesse, Are here all thy children? And he said, There remaineth yet the youngest, and, behold, he keepeth the sheep. And Samuel said unto Jesse, Send and fetch him: for we will not sit down till he come hither.*
    > *And he sent, and brought him in. Now he was ruddy, and withal of a beautiful countenance, and goodly to look to. And the LORD said, Arise, anoint him: for this is he.*
    > *Then Samuel took the horn of oil, and anointed him in the midst of his brethren: and the Spirit of the LORD came upon David from that day forward. So Samuel rose up, and went to Ramah."*
    > 1 Samuel 16:11-13

ONE // FINDING THE VOICE OF GOD

Defending sheep prepared him to defend a nation.

- **MATTHEW (LEVI)**

Sitting at the tax collector's table when the Lord Jesus called him.

> *"And as Jesus passed forth from thence, He saw a man, named Matthew, sitting at the receipt of custom: and He saith unto him, Follow Me. And he arose, and followed Him."*
> Matthew 9:9

Grace interrupted him at the very place of corruption.

- **PAUL (SAUL)**

On the road to Damascus, persecuting the church, when the voice of the Lord Jesus arrested him.

> *"And as he journeyed, he came near Damascus: and suddenly there shined round about him a light from heaven:*
> *And he fell to the earth, and heard a voice saying unto him, Saul, Saul, why persecutest thou Me?*
> *And he said, Who art Thou, Lord? And the Lord said, I am Jesus whom thou persecutest: it is hard for thee to kick against the pricks.*
> *And he trembling and astonished said, Lord, what wilt Thou have me to do? And the Lord said unto him, Arise, and go into the city, and it shall be told thee what thou must do."*
> Acts 9:3-6

Even misdirected zeal was redeemed into apostleship.

These examples reveal a prophetic pattern: God's voice often finds you while you are functioning in what you know, so that He can reveal what you were truly born for.

Purpose does not discard your skills, experiences, nor even your past; it redeems and redefines them. The nets of Peter, the staff of Moses, the oxen of Elisha, the scrolls of Paul…everything becomes a tool in the hands of God once His voice calls it into alignment with eternal purpose.

THE VOICE FOR NATIONS

It is important to note God's voice is not limited to His covenant people. Even unbelievers can hear Him when their role intersects with His eternal plan.

- **PHARAOH IN JOSEPH'S DAY**

Though he did not serve God, Pharaoh received dreams of the famine. Why? Because his rule was the platform upon which Israel would be preserved.

> *"And Joseph said unto Pharaoh, The dream of Pharaoh is one: God hath shewed Pharaoh what he is about to do."*
> Genesis 41:25

- **NEBUCHADNEZZAR OF BABYLON**

He was arrogant and idolatrous, yet he received visions, warnings, and even a dream of the eternal kingdom that would outlast his own. God spoke, because his reign was connected to the destiny of the Hebrew exiles.

> *"Daniel answered in the presence of the king, and said, The secret which the king hath demanded cannot the wise men, the astrologers, the magicians, the soothsayers, shew unto the king;*
> *But there is a God in heaven that revealeth secrets, and maketh known to the king Nebuchadnezzar what shall be in the latter days. Thy dream, and the visions of thy head upon thy bed, are these;*
> *As for thee, O king, thy thoughts came into thy mind upon thy bed, what should come to pass hereafter: and He that revealeth secrets maketh known to thee what shall come to pass."*
> Daniel 2:27-29

These examples prove that God's voice is not confined to faith but to function. If a person or a nation stands in the pathway of His purpose, He will speak.

THE VOICE AT THE ALTAR

Consider Abraham. By bringing Lot along with him, he caused delays in the unfolding of God's promise. Yet Abraham discovered a key: whenever he returned to the altar, the voice returned as well.

> *"And he went on his journeys from the south even to Bethel, unto the place where his tent had been at the beginning, between Bethel and Hai;*
> *Unto the place of the altar, which he had made there at the first:*

and there Abram called on the name of the LORD."
Genesis 13:3-4

The altar is the place of alignment. When we drift, the altar restores clarity. When distractions cloud our journey, the altar becomes the compass. It is here that God's voice reaffirms purpose, realigns direction, and restores clarity. If you feel the silence of God, ask yourself: when was the last time you returned to the altar of prayer, worship, and surrender?

A PROPHETIC WARNING TO SEEKERS

Now, hear this warning by the Spirit: do not run to seek mentors, fathers, or mothers in the faith before you have sought God for your own purpose. So many dishonor coverings, not because those coverings failed, but because they themselves never discerned why they were there. They drain the grace of spiritual parents, then grow offended when their immaturity is revealed. Many who were once destined for greatness shipwrecked because they pursued titles over purpose and desired recognition more than revelation.

Beloved, do not fall in love with titles. Fall in love with the functionality of your divine calling. Fast and pray without preconceived ideas. Lay aside ambition. Let the Lord Jesus Christ Himself reveal the assignment of your life. Only then should you seek guidance, for then you will honor fathers and mothers in the faith rightly, and their pouring will not be wasted.

ONE // FINDING THE VOICE OF GOD

THE ANCHOR OF GOD'S VOICE

This is the key, simple and eternal: when you are in your purpose, you will not miss the voice of God. His voice will convict you in sin, restore you in failure, guide you in confusion, and affirm you in alignment. Even in silence, His voice will wait for you at the altar.

Return to calling. Align with purpose. Fall in love with functionality, not titles. In that place, you will find that His voice is not only clear, it is constant, transitioning you from one dimension to another.

> *"And thine ears shall hear a word behind thee, saying, This is the way, walk ye in it, when ye turn to the right hand, and when ye turn to the left."*
> Isaiah 30:21

Prayer for the Discovery of Purpose

Father, in the name of Your Son Jesus Christ, I thank You for calling me into life with intention and purpose. I confess that without Your voice, I cannot walk in light, and without Your direction, I cannot fulfill the reason You sent me into this world.

Lord, open my ears once more. Cause me to hear the echo of Your Spirit that convicts, guides, and restores. Where I have walked outside of Your will, bring me back into the path of purpose. Where I have been blinded by ambition or distracted by titles, strip away every false desire until only Your eternal plan remains.

Holy Spirit, breathe into me the revelation of my divine assignment. Let the altar of prayer be my compass, and let Your word confirm my steps. Align my heart with the function You gave me before the foundation of the world.

I renounce confusion and silence, and I embrace clarity and direction. I declare that I was born with a divine purpose, and by Your mercy, I shall not miss it. Lord Jesus, guide me, correct me, and keep me within the borders of my destiny.

Let my ears hear the voice that says, "This is the way, walk in it." Let my life resound with the purpose You ordained, that I may glorify Your name all my days.

Amen.

Two
DESIRING THE PROPHETIC

TWO // DESIRING THE PROPHETIC

"Follow after charity, and desire spiritual gifts, but rather that ye may prophesy."
1 Corinthians 14:1

It is true that we can and should desire spiritual gifts as the Scriptures declare, including the prophetic. However, before we pursue the gifts of the Spirit, we must understand the laws that govern the realm of gifts. Spiritual gifts do not operate by emotion, ambition, or entitlement; they are governed by spiritual principles, divine order, and eternal purpose.

Understanding what God has made available, as well as being able to separate what is not meant for us, is essential. This wisdom protects us from deception and positions us to receive what the Lord has truly offered us through His Son, Jesus Christ. We are not to chase gifts blindly; we must pursue with revelation, with humility, and with alignment, for only then can we truly receive, carry, and manifest the prophetic with purity, integrity, and supernatural power.

THE PROBLEM OF MISUNDERSTANDING

Over the years, I have heard many discussions surrounding the prophetic. Although some are sincere, many are misguided. It grieves me to say this, but much of what circulates in the Body of Christ concerning the prophetic is not rooted in true spiritual understanding.

Do not teach what you do not understand. Please hear me by the Spirit of God. The failure to comply with this principle has caused great confusion in the Church, especially regarding spiritual gifts and the prophetic ministry.

Many attempt to handle the things of the Spirit with unwashed hands and unprepared hearts. Most who attempt to teach the prophetic are neither prophets nor truly prophetic. They speak from borrowed information, not personal revelation. They echo what they have heard, not what they have received from the mouth of God Himself. Thus, the prophetic has been diluted by carnal interpretations, academic debates, and denominational politics, until in many places, it has become a form without power. But I thank God that He is raising for Himself true vessels, birthed by the Spirit and sent forth for His own will.

THE THREE GIVERS OF GIFTS

In the divine order of heaven, there are three great Givers of gifts: The Father, the Son, and the Holy Spirit. Each gives according to His nature, and all the gifts flow together to build the Body of Christ and establish the Kingdom of God.

THE GIFT OF GOD THE FATHER

The greatest and most important gift from the Father is not a thing, it is **a Person**: Jesus Christ, His holy and only begotten Son.

> *"For God so loved the world, that He gave His only begotten Son, that whosoever believeth in Him should not perish, but have everlasting life.*
> John 3:16

TWO // DESIRING THE PROPHETIC

The gift of the Father was His Son. Through Christ, all other blessings and gifts flow. Without Jesus, there is no access to anything divine, no existence at all.

> *"In the beginning was the Word, and the Word was with God, and the Word was God.*
> *The same was in the beginning with God.*
> *All things were made by Him; and without Him was not any thing made that was made.*
> John 1:1-3

> *"For by Him were all things created, that are in heaven, and that are in earth, visible and invisible, whether they be thrones, or dominions, or principalities, or powers: all things were created by Him, and for Him:*
> *And He is before all things, and by Him all things consist."*
> Colossians 1:16-17

Christ is the foundation of every gift and every calling. He is the Father's great offering to the world.

THE GIFTS OF THE SON

The Son, Jesus Christ, is the manifested image of the invisible God, clothed in flesh.

> *"Who being the brightness of His glory, and the express image of His person, and upholding all things by the word of His power, when He had by Himself purged our sins, sat down on the right*

hand of the Majesty on high."
Hebrews 1:3

Having redeemed His people, Christ gives **gifts to His Church** alone:

"Wherefore He saith, When He ascended up on high, He led captivity captive, and gave gifts unto men."
Ephesians 4:8

These gifts are not talents but living vessels:

- Apostles
- Prophets
- Evangelists
- Pastors
- Teachers

"For the perfecting of the saints, for the work of the ministry, for the edifying of the body of Christ."
Ephesians 4:12

These gifts will remain until the Church attains full maturity in Christ.

CONFRONTING THE ATTACK AGAINST GOD'S GIFTS

A demonic deception whispers: *"You don't need anyone but your Bible and Jesus."* This is rebellion in disguise. Jesus established the fivefold ministry; rejecting God's gifts is rejecting His design.

> *"My sheep hear my voice, and I know them, and they follow me."*
> John 10:27

Fear of deception will grow, but true sons of God will arise, and their light will drive out darkness. Though human vessels err, their errors don't nullify their divine assignments. When a vessel corrupts the calling, the Lord Himself will deal with them, as Gamaliel warned:

> *"And now I say unto you, Refrain from these men, and let them alone: for if this counsel or this work be of men, it will come to nought:*
> *But if it be of God, ye cannot overthrow it; lest haply ye be found even to fight against God."*
> Acts 5:38-39

THE GIFTS OF THE HOLY SPIRIT

The Spirit's gifts are **manifestations of divine abilities** operating through believers, not people.

> *"But the manifestation of the Spirit is given to every man to profit withal."*
> 1 Corinthians 12:7

Know this: there are more than nine gifts; the Spirit is not confined to human tradition.

MANIFESTATION GIFTS
(1 CORINTHIANS 12:8-10)

- Word of Wisdom
- Word of Knowledge
- Faith
- Gifts of Healings
- Working of Miracles
- Prophecy
- Discerning of Spirits
- Different Kinds of Tongues
- Interpretation of Tongues

MOTIVATIONAL GIFTS
(ROMANS 12:6-8)

- Prophecy
- Ministry (Serving)
- Teaching
- Exhortation
- Giving
- Leading
- Mercy

ADMINISTRATIVE GIFTS AND OPERATIONS
(1 CORINTHIANS 12:28)

- Apostles
- Prophets
- Teachers
- Miracles

TWO // DESIRING THE PROPHETIC

- Gifts of Healings
- Helps
- Governments
- Diversities of Tongues

To clarify, Apostles, Prophets and Teachers here refer to men gifted with spiritual and administrative capabilities, appointed by local leadership. They may function in these roles without carrying the foundational office of Ephesians 4:11.

OTHER SPECIFIC GIFTS

- Evangelism (Ephesians 4:11)
- Pastoral Grace (Jeremiah 3:5)
- Interpretation of Dreams (Daniel 1:17)
- Hospitality (1 Peter 4:9-10)
- Celibacy (1 Corinthians 7:7)
- Supernatural Endurance – Martyrdom (Revelation 2:10)

The Spirit gives freely, distributing as He wills according to divine purpose.

A WORD OF WISDOM

If there is one truth I pray you carry from this chapter, it is this:

only the gifts of the Holy Spirit can be desired. The offices of Apostle, Prophet, Evangelist, Pastor, and Teacher, are given by Christ alone.

Fivefold ministers are not volunteers; they were born for that purpose, ordained by grace before time began. I cannot justify why or how I was born a prophet; it is only by election through grace.

Desiring spiritual function does not make you lesser. *Greatness in the Kingdom is service*, as Jesus taught:

"But he that is greatest among you shall be your servant."
Matthew 23:11

Desire gifts, serve with love, and let the Lord determine your assignment.

TWO // DESIRING THE PROPHETIC

Prayer

    Father, in the name of Jesus Christ, Your holy Son, I thank You for Your love. I thank You for choosing me as a vessel to bless Your people.

    Holy Spirit, help me be a faithful steward of every gift, and may I always glorify You as I win souls to Your Kingdom. Father of all spirits, awaken my gifts today and empower me.

    In Jesus' mighty name, Amen.

Three
PURITY OF THE SOUL

THREE // PURITY OF THE SOUL

"Blessed are the pure in heart: for they shall see God."
Matthew 5:8

Purity is one of the most vital keys to flowing in the prophetic. A heart that is clean, still, and unclouded becomes a vessel through which the voice of God can clearly pass. On the other hand, a person who is opinionated, leaning too heavily on their own thoughts or understanding, will often distort the message. They begin to mix the divine with the carnal, inserting self into what should be Spirit.

The soul, in its natural state, is rarely quiet. It is usually restless, as it is always analyzing, questioning, and trying to comprehend. This is why Adam and Eve were so easily deceived in Genesis chapter 3. The soul is not all-knowing; it is not all-wise. It hungers for understanding, and in that hunger, it can be led astray. The soul's desire to "know" apart from God becomes its greatest vulnerability, and unless it is purified and subdued, meaning, unless it yields to the Spirit, it becomes a breeding ground for corruption.

Only the pure in heart shall see God; not just in eternity, but even now, in the realm of divine encounters, visions, and prophetic insight. It is the very nature of the soul to desire control. The soul craves authority, influence, and independence. This is why Satan's deception in the garden was so effective. He didn't present Eve with a blatant rebellion; he offered her something that resonated with the soul's hidden desire: to be in charge, to be like God, and to no longer need Him.

"For God doth know that in the day ye eat thereof, then your eyes shall be opened, and ye shall be as gods, knowing good and evil."
Genesis 3:5

Satan's words were calculated. He understood the soul's

weakness by its longing to grasp, to know, and to govern itself without guidance. He planted the idea that God was withholding something, that divine boundaries were a threat to personal growth, and that freedom meant separation from divine dependence. Yet what the enemy offered was not growth but corruption.

God never intended to withhold wisdom or maturity from man. His plan was always for the soul to grow under His guidance, like a child maturing under the watchful care of a parent. The soul, like a child, cannot govern itself well. Without the Holy Spirit, our divine Teacher and Guardian, it becomes unstable, easily deceived, and ultimately destructive.

True prophetic sensitivity can only flow through a soul that has been submitted and purified, a soul that has relinquished control and embraced the Spirit as its sole source of wisdom and authority.

When we begin to peer into the spirit realm, which many call the world of spirits, it's important to make a distinction: not all spirits are angels, and not all angels are the same. The term *spirit* encompasses more than just angels and demons. God, in His infinite creativity, has formed a variety of beings; some with flesh and some without, some purely spiritual, others angelic in nature, and some that exist in between. This foundational understanding is critical for those who are called to walk deeply in the prophetic.

Let me give you a simple, yet powerful, example:

> *"And whereas the king saw a watcher and an holy one coming down from heaven, and saying, Hew the tree down, and destroy it; yet leave the stump of the roots thereof in the earth, even with a band of iron and brass, in the tender grass of the field; and let it be wet with the dew of heaven, and let his portion be with the beasts of the field, till seven times pass over him."*
> Daniel 4:23

THREE // PURITY OF THE SOUL

Prophet Daniel makes a careful distinction in this verse: he speaks of *a watcher* and *a holy one*; two beings, not one. One may ask, aren't all angels holy? The answer, according to Scripture, is yes:

> *"When the Son of Man shall come in His glory, and all the holy angels with Him, then shall He sit upon the throne of His glory."*
> Matthew 25:31

> *"...when He shall come in His own glory, and in His Father's, and of the holy angels."*
> Luke 9:26

Clearly, angels are holy by design. So why then does Daniel distinguish between a "watcher" and a "holy one"? Because not all watchers are the same as the holy angels who dwell continually in the heaven of heavens.

Watchers are a unique class of spiritual beings. They are both spirit and flesh. We see this hinted at in Genesis 6, where the "sons of God," a phrase often interpreted as referring to watchers, took wives from among human women and bore children who became giants, the Nephilim. This means that watchers carried DNA and had reproductive capacity, something not attributed to the holy angels of heaven.

> *"For when they shall rise from the dead, they neither marry, nor are given in marriage; but are as the angels which are in heaven."*
> Mark 12:25

This verse reinforces a key point: the angels who dwell in the heaven of heavens are not given to marriage, nor do they possess the capacity for sexual union. This means that any being that does have such capacity must have originated from a different realm or dimension within the heavens, and not the highest heaven, where God's throne resides.

Therefore, when Daniel refers to the "holy one," he is referring to a being from the heaven of heavens. The "watcher" is something else; though still angelic, they are not of the same order. The watcher operates from a lower heavenly realm, with a different function, and evidently, a different nature. These truths about spirits are essential in understanding the soul, especially how it can be corrupted.

They also begin to answer a critical question: *How did Satan know exactly how to corrupt the human soul?* The Bible does not explicitly state that angels possess souls in the same way humans do. However, when we observe the behavior of angels throughout Scripture, we find that they express emotion, execute will, and even respond with what seems like personality and depth. These attributes of mind, will, and emotion, are the very components that make up the human soul. While the language may differ in the spiritual realm, it is possible that angelic beings possess something akin to a soul; perhaps not in the exact form as ours, but with similar faculties.

Lucifer, before his fall, was a cherub; that is a high-ranking angel from the heaven of heavens. When we examine his fall, we begin to see the same vulnerabilities and emotional patterns that humans battle today. This gives us a clue: the corruption of the soul begins internally, in that which one chooses to meditate upon.

> *"Thine heart was lifted up because of thy beauty, thou hast corrupted thy wisdom by reason of thy brightness..."*
> Ezekiel 28:17

This verse reveals several powerful truths. First, Lucifer had a heart. Ezekiel, speaking by divine revelation, acknowledges it. The heart in Scripture is not just the seat of emotion; it is the core of thought, will, and intent. God does not create any being without the ability to choose. Why? Because love demands choice. Without choice, there can be no love. Second, his heart was lifted up. This is pride. The moment he began to exalt himself, iniquity was born in him. And where did that iniquity begin? In his imagination. Third, he corrupted his wisdom. Meaning, he still retained knowledge, but now used it for deception. Satan is not without intelligence. In fact, he is creative; but his creativity is twisted. He does not have the power to create life; he only possesses the skill to imitate, distort, and pervert what God has made.

This is why Satan was able to corrupt Eve. He understood the structure of the soul because he had one. He knew how desire works. He knew how pride stirs. He knew how imagination opens the door to rebellion. He also knew that once the soul starts to drift from divine dependence, it becomes vulnerable to suggestion. Lucifer's fall was the prototype. Man's fall followed the same pattern.

We can drive this truth even deeper by returning to the words of Lucifer in Isaiah.

> *"For thou hast said in thine heart, I will ascend into heaven, I will exalt my throne above the stars of God: I will sit also upon the mount of the congregation, in the sides of the north:*
> *I will ascend above the heights of the clouds; I will be like the most High."*
> Isaiah 14:13-14

Five times, Lucifer declares, "I will." Each declaration reveals a being consumed by inner vision. He *saw* himself exalted. He *envisioned* a throne above God's stars. He imagined himself seated in divine authority. These were not idle thoughts; they were the fruit of an active mind, a desiring heart, and a corrupted imagination.

This confirms that spirit beings, particularly angelic ones like cherubim, possess not only intelligence and function, but also will, imagination, and emotion. They are not mechanical messengers. They feel deeply. They long. They respond. And when their affections become self-centered, even celestial glory can become fuel for pride.

Lucifer's fall was not merely intellectual or volitional, it was emotional. His heart was lifted up. He became infatuated with his own beauty. He was moved by pride and stirred by desire. The emotions once designed to glorify God turned inward, igniting obsession with self. Emotion, when unguarded by humility and disconnected from truth, becomes the fire that births rebellion.

Lucifer's sin was not reaction; it was intention. He meditated on self-exaltation until it became iniquity. He imagined glory without submission, and desired elevation without reverence. Therein lies the mirror for the human soul: the very faculties that led to Lucifer's downfall, the will, desire, imagination and emotion, are all alive in us. If not brought under the lordship of Christ, these gifts can become gateways to the same corruption that cast a cherub out of heaven.

The Lord continues in Isaiah 14 by not only exposing Lucifer's inner rebellion, but also declaring the nature of his judgment:

> *"Yet thou shalt be brought down to hell, to the sides of the pit. They that see thee shall narrowly look upon thee, and consider thee, saying, Is this the man that made the earth to tremble, that did shake kingdoms?"*
> Isaiah 14:15-16

Before judgment comes in the form of fire, chains, or eternal torment, it comes as humiliation. God does not strip in private; He exposes in justice. He said, *"I will lay thee before kings, that they may behold*

THREE // PURITY OF THE SOUL

thee" (*Ezekiel 28:17*). Lucifer, who sought to exalt himself above the congregation in heaven, is made a spectacle before rulers on earth. The irony is divine: the one who desired to sit on a throne above the stars is now stared at, mocked, and remembered in shame.

> *"All they that know thee among the people shall be astonished at thee: thou shalt be a terror, and never shalt thou be any more."*
> Ezekiel 28:19

Before his fire is eternal, his fall is emotional. Before he is judged in torment, he is crushed in pride. Lucifer's first punishment was not chains; it was humiliation.

This is why emotional warfare is so real in the lives of prophetic people. Satan was wounded in his emotions first; his pride was shattered, his beauty mocked, and his glory stripped. Consequently, one of his chief weapons is emotional corruption: offense, insecurity, rejection, bitterness, and pride. He sows these into the souls of men and women of God because they are the very tools that destroyed him.

God Himself declares that He has a heart. This is a truth that reveals the soul-nature within the very being of the uncreated Creator. We find this striking revelation in Genesis 6:

> *"And it repented the Lord that He had made man on the earth, and it grieved Him at His heart."*
> Genesis 6:6

This is an extraordinary verse. It is one of the earliest moments in Scripture where we are invited into the emotional world of God. Moses, caught up in divine encounter on Mount Sinai, records this moment as part of the origin story of creation, and what he reveals is astounding: *God feels deeply.*

From this single verse, we gather several divine truths.

1. GOD CAN EXPERIENCE HEARTBREAK

The word *grieved* here is profound. It doesn't just imply disappointment; it speaks of pain, sorrow, and emotional weight. The Creator felt heartbreak because of the corruption of man. This is not weakness, but love expressed through divine vulnerability.

"How oft did they provoke him in the wilderness, and grieve him in the desert!"
Psalm 78:40

"And grieve not the holy Spirit of God, whereby ye are sealed unto the day of redemption."
Ephesians 4:30

Only one who possesses emotion, not random force, can grieve. God grieves because He cares.

2. GOD CAN EXPRESS REGRET EVEN WHILE BEING ALL-KNOWING

The phrase *"it repented the Lord..."* does not mean that God made a mistake. Rather, it reveals the emotional cost of granting free will. Even though God knew the outcome, He still felt the weight of that choice in real time. This shows us that God is not emotionally detached from His creation.

"It repenteth Me that I have set up Saul to be king: for he is

turned back from following Me, and hath not performed My commandments. And it grieved Samuel; and he cried unto the LORD all night."
1 Samuel 15:11

God knew Saul's end from the beginning, yet He still expressed sorrow. This is because love always hopes, and love always feels.

3. GOD HAS A WILL AND DESIRES FOR US TO ALIGN WITH IT

God's will is neither robotic nor static; it is relational. He responds to how we respond.

"And be not conformed to this world: but be ye transformed by the renewing of your mind, that ye may prove what is that good, and acceptable, and perfect, will of God."
Romans 12:2

"For this is the will of God, even your sanctification, that ye should abstain from fornication."
1 Thessalonians 4:3

The will of God is personal, intentional, and purposeful. He doesn't just decree, He desires. He invites us into partnership with His will.

4. GOD CAN BE PLEASED OR DISPLEASED

Throughout Scripture God receives offerings and sacrifices with joy, or rejects them with sorrow and at times even anger, based on the condition of the heart that offers them.

"And Abel, he also brought of the firstlings of his flock and of the fat thereof. And the LORD had respect unto Abel and to his offering:
But unto Cain and to his offering He had not respect. And Cain was very wroth, and his countenance fell."
Genesis 4:4-5

"To what purpose is the multitude of your sacrifices unto Me? saith the LORD: I am full of the burnt offerings of rams, and the fat of fed beasts; and I delight not in the blood of bullocks, or of lambs, or of he goats."
Isaiah 1:11

"But to do good and to communicate forget not: for with such sacrifices God is well pleased."
Hebrews 13:16

God is not indifferent. He is emotionally, spiritually, and relationally engaged with His creation. We feel, because He first felt. We choose, because He first willed. We grieve, because He too can be grieved. To know the will of God is to understand His heart. And to walk in His Spirit is to respond in kind; that is, to love what He loves, to reject what He rejects, and to pursue what pleases Him.

God does not merely desire obedience, He desires love. This is because true obedience is not mechanical but emotional. Jesus said:

"Jesus said unto him, Thou shalt love the Lord thy God with all

THREE // PURITY OF THE SOUL

thy heart, and with all thy soul, and with all thy mind."
Matthew 22:37

This is not just a call to action, but a call to emotional alignment. God wants our obedience to be saturated with affection. The command is not simply to do what He says, but to love Him fully, with the totality of our emotions, will, and intellect.

This is where much of the modern Church has gone numb. There is a great deficiency of emotion, and that not in expression, but in purity. Many obey externally but feel nothing internally. Their hearts are calloused, their compassion dulled. They are driven by law, not love. As a result, they misrepresent the God they serve.

This is why many ministers today proclaim judgment without tears. They thunder warnings from pulpits, but cannot weep for the lost. They declare consequences, but cannot discern the mercy of the Father's heart. Their emotions have become defiled, and in losing emotional purity, they have lost prophetic sensitivity.

This is exactly what we see in the story of Jonah the prophet. Jonah's story is often simplified as one of disobedience, yet it is far more complex and deeply emotional. From the beginning, Jonah knew God's heart. He understood that the Lord was not sending him to Nineveh to destroy the people, but to bring them to repentance. This is why he fled to Tarshish. He wasn't running from the task; rather, he was resisting the outcome. He said it plainly:

"I knew that thou art a gracious God, and merciful, slow to anger, and of great kindness, and repentest thee of the evil."
Jonah 4:2

But after being thrown into the sea and swallowed by the great fish, something shifted in Jonah. The trauma of the storm and the depths of the ocean caused him to reinterpret the assignment. He began to believe that perhaps God really did intend to destroy Nineveh, and that the judgment he had resisted was, in fact, final.

In response to all that he had experienced, Jonah obeyed outwardly. He delivered the message, but his heart was still troubled, and his emotions were wounded. He climbed a hill, sat in the heat, and waited; not to celebrate revival, but to see if God would truly destroy the city. And when it didn't happen, he was disappointed; not just because the city was spared, but because he had suffered for something God never truly intended to carry out. He felt betrayed. He had endured the storm, the sea, and the belly of the fish, only to declare a word that would not be fulfilled.

> *"Therefore now, O Lord, take, I beseech thee, my life from me; for it is better for me to die than to live."*
> Jonah 4:3

Jonah was not angry because he didn't understand God. On the contrary, he was angry because he did. He felt used, perhaps even mocked by the process. But God, in His love, did not rebuke him harshly. Instead, He taught him gently, prophetically, and with great wisdom. The gourd, the worm, and the scorching wind were not punishments but parables. God was showing Jonah: *"You have pity for a plant that lived for a moment. Should I not have mercy on a people I created, who do not know their left hand from their right?"*

> *"Then said the LORD, Thou hast had pity on the gourd, for the which thou hast not laboured, neither madest it grow; which came up in a night, and perished in a night:*
> *And should not I spare Nineveh, that great city, wherein are more than sixscore thousand persons that cannot discern between their*

THREE // PURITY OF THE SOUL

right hand and their left hand; and also much cattle?"
Jonah 4:10-11

Jonah's story reveals that emotional confusion can cloud prophetic understanding. He knew God's nature, but the pain of the process caused him to doubt it; that doubt made him misread the intent behind his assignment.

This is the danger when obedience is disconnected from emotional purity. A prophet can declare what God says, yet misunderstand what God means. They can preach truth, but miss intention. They can speak judgment, when God's heart is weeping for mercy. God was not correcting Jonah's message. God was correcting Jonah's heart.

God does not just desire action, He also desires attitude. He wants what we give, but He also wants *how* we give it. The posture of the heart matters.

> *"Every man according as he purposeth in his heart, so let him give; not grudgingly, or of necessity: for God loveth a cheerful giver."*
> 2 Corinthians 9:7

This verse reveals that, to God, giving is not just about generosity but also about joy. God loves the giver whose heart is free, whose emotions are pure, and who gives out of love rather than guilt or fear. The same is true for everything else we do:

> *"And whatsoever ye do, do it heartily, as to the Lord, and not unto men."*
> Colossians 3:23

> *"With good will doing service, as to the Lord, and not to men."*
> Ephesians 6:7

Why does God care so deeply about our motives and emotions? Because purity of heart begins with emotional purification. Many believers today love God with their mouths, but carry hearts poisoned by past trauma. They sing in worship, but are harsh in character. They tithe, but carry bitterness. They serve in church, but cannot love their neighbor. Why? Because their emotions have not been healed. Some can no longer give freely to God because they were once manipulated by corrupt ministers. Some cannot receive a prophetic word because a false prophet once misled or wounded them, so now, they've closed their hearts not just to people, but to the voice of the Lord Himself. As a result, worship becomes mechanical. Giving becomes obligatory. Service becomes lifeless. They go through the motions, but their hearts are far from the flame of divine love.

Hear me by the Spirit of God: this ought not to be. God is calling His people to a place of complete emotional restoration. It is through the emotions that we begin to truly discern the heart of God, but only when they have been purified and submitted to the Spirit. You cannot know His compassion if you cannot feel your own. You cannot carry His burden for the lost if your own heart is numb. And you cannot walk in prophetic accuracy if your soul is still ruled by the pain of yesterday.

Emotional purity is not weakness, it is spiritual strength. Emotional purity is the gateway to intimacy with God and clarity in the prophetic. It is how we move from cold obedience to fiery love where our giving, our worship, and our words flow from a heart that is healed, whole, and aligned with the heart of the Father.

We know that the soul is immaterial, just as the spirit is, though they are distinct in nature and function. While the soul is composed of

THREE // PURITY OF THE SOUL

the mind, will, and emotions, the spirit contains conscience, fellowship, and intuition, the parts of us designed to commune directly with God. The soul is the seat of personality and choice. The spirit is the seat of divine connection and revelation.

Now, while the soul and spirit are separate, they are meant to be in union, not contradiction. This is why Scripture speaks of both a carnal mind and a spiritual mind:

> *"For to be carnally minded is death; but to be spiritually minded is life and peace.*
> *Because the carnal mind is enmity against God: for it is not subject to the law of God, neither indeed can be."*
> Romans 8:6-7

> *"But the natural man receiveth not the things of the Spirit of God: for they are foolishness unto him: neither can he know them, because they are spiritually discerned."*
> 1 Corinthians 2:14

These verses show us that the mind, which is the most active part of the soul, can either war against the spirit or come under its influence. It can either follow flesh or become one with Spirit. This means that soul purity is not just about resisting sin; it is about full alignment with the spirit-man. Soul purity is possible when the mind is renewed, the will is surrendered, and the emotions are sanctified; the soul becomes joined to the spirit man who is already in communion with God.

This is what Paul meant when he wrote:

> *"And be not conformed to this world: but be ye transformed by the renewing of your mind, that ye may prove what*

> *is that good, and acceptable, and perfect, will of God."*
> Romans 12:2

And again:

> *"And the very God of peace sanctify you wholly; and I pray God your whole spirit and soul and body be preserved blameless unto the coming of our Lord Jesus Christ."*
> 1 Thessalonians 5:23

When the soul is purified, it no longer fights the spirit; it flows with it. The renewed mind begins to process like the spirit. The submitted will begins to obey like the spirit. The healed emotions begin to feel what the Spirit of God feels. That is when emotional and soul purity is complete: when the soul has become a vessel that no longer speaks for itself, but echoes the voice of the spirit. It is no longer divided but united, no longer torn between the flesh and Spirit; it is fused with the inner man in communion with God.

How does emotional healing and purity happen? It begins with surrender, not with strength. It is not the product of trying harder, but of yielding more deeply to the Spirit of God. Emotional healing happens when the soul is laid bare before the Lord; all the pain, pride, shame, fear, and bitterness are brought into the light of His presence.

> *"The Lord is nigh unto them that are of a broken heart; and saveth such as be of a contrite spirit."*
> Psalm 34:18

God does not reject the broken, He draws near to them. He restores by presence, not by pressure. He doesn't ask us to pretend we're whole; He invites us to admit that we are not.

THREE // PURITY OF THE SOUL

Consider Peter, the bold disciple who swore he would never deny Jesus. When he failed and denied the Lord three times, the emotional wound was so deep that Scripture says he went out and wept bitterly.

> *"And the Lord turned, and looked upon Peter. And Peter remembered the word of the Lord, how He had said unto him, Before the cock crow, thou shalt deny Me thrice.*
> *And Peter went out, and wept bitterly."*
> Luke 22:61-62

This was not surface regret; it was soul collapse. Shame had crushed him and his confidence was shattered. However, the Lord Jesus had already seen his fall and made provision for his restoration, not just his forgiveness. After His resurrection, the Master appeared to Peter and asked him three times, *"Do you love Me?"*

> *"So when they had dined, Jesus saith to Simon Peter, Simon, son of Jonas, lovest thou me more than these? He saith unto Him, Yea, Lord; thou knowest that I love Thee. He saith unto him, Feed my lambs.*
> *He saith to him again the second time, Simon, son of Jonas, lovest thou Me? He saith unto Him, Yea, Lord; Thou knowest that I love Thee. He saith unto him, Feed my sheep.*
> *He saith unto him the third time, Simon, son of Jonas, lovest thou me? Peter was grieved because He said unto him the third time, Lovest thou me? And he said unto Him, Lord, Thou knowest all things; Thou knowest that I love Thee. Jesus saith unto him, Feed my sheep."*
> John 21:15-17

This was not an interrogation; this was a healing. The Lord was reopening the wound, not to hurt Peter again, but in order to heal it at its root. Each question uprooted the shame, each answer re-established trust, and each time Christ responded, *"Feed My sheep,"* He was restoring Peter's identity and commissioning him afresh. Peter didn't only recover, he became stronger, because the place of his greatest pain became the platform for his greatest calling.

This is emotional healing:

- Not avoiding the past, but facing it in the presence of Christ.
- Not suppressing the pain, but letting the Holy Spirit rewrite its story.
- Not trying to be strong, but learning to be surrendered.

We see this again in Joseph, who was betrayed by his own brothers, falsely accused, and forgotten in prison. Yet when he rose to power in Egypt and his brothers stood before him, Joseph wept not from bitterness, but from the release of years of divine healing.

> *"And Joseph said unto his brethren, Come near to me, I pray you. And they came near. And he said, I am Joseph your brother, whom ye sold into Egypt.*
> *Now therefore be not grieved, nor angry with yourselves, that ye sold me hither: for God did send me before you to preserve life."*
> Genesis 45:4-5

Joseph didn't simply forgive; he had been emotionally healed. He could speak peace because God had worked peace into him.

Then there is David, the psalmist and king who poured out his emotions before God time and again:

THREE // PURITY OF THE SOUL

"Create in me a clean heart, O God; and renew a right spirit within me."
Psalm 51:10

"I am weary with my groaning; all the night make I my bed to swim; I water my couch with my tears."
Psalm 6:6

David didn't hide his emotions, he brought them into worship; and through worship, God purified them. Emotional purity happens when:

1. WE CONFESS, NOT CONCEAL, OUR PAIN.

"Confess your faults one to another, and pray one for another, that ye may be healed. The effectual fervent prayer of a righteous man availeth much."
James 5:16

2. WE ALLOW THE HOLY SPIRIT TO SEARCH AND REVEAL WHAT'S BROKEN.

"Search me, O God, and know my heart: try me, and know my thoughts."
Psalm 139:23

3. WE FORGIVE TRULY AND FULLY THOSE WHO WOUNDED US.

"Judge not, and ye shall not be judged: condemn not, and ye shall

not be condemned: forgive, and ye shall be forgiven."
Luke 6:37

4. WE REPLACE LIES WITH TRUTH THROUGH THE WORD.

"And be not conformed to this world: but be ye transformed by the renewing of your mind, that ye may prove what is that good, and acceptable, and perfect, will of God."
Romans 12:2

5. WE WALK IN INTIMACY WITH THE LORD, NOT PERFORMANCE.

"He restoreth my soul: He leadeth me in the paths of righteousness for His name's sake."
Psalm 23:3

God is not just healing actions; He is healing affections. He is not just cleansing hands; He is cleansing hearts. When the soul is healed, the emotions purified, and the spirit aligned, we become vessels that can truly carry the weight of the prophetic, the love of God, and the wisdom of heaven.

Four
THE SIN THAT SILENCES GOD

FOUR // THE SIN THAT SILENCES GOD

There is a great deal of misinformation when it comes to hearing the voice of God in connection to sin. While it is absolutely true that God our Father hates sin, the deeper revelation is this: there is only one sin that truly severs creation from the voice of God, and that is the sin of pride.

Pride is not just another sin; it is the root of all rebellion. It is the original fracture, the very first defiance that attempted to rise against the throne of God. To understand the severing power of pride, we must journey back to its origin, found not in humanity, but in the heavenly realm. Before Adam ever sinned, iniquity was found in one who once stood in radiant perfection.

Ezekiel 28:14-19 gives us a glimpse into the fall of Lucifer, the anointed cherub who once walked among the stones of fire, in the very presence of God. He was not merely present in Heaven; he was established by God, positioned on the holy mountain, clothed in beauty, and crowned with divine purpose.

> *"Thou art the anointed cherub that covereth; and I have set thee so: thou wast upon the holy mountain of God; thou hast walked up and down in the midst of the stones of fire.*
> *Thou wast perfect in thy ways from the day that thou wast created, till iniquity was found in thee."*
> Ezekiel 28:14-15

Lucifer's fall did not begin with an external act; it began with an internal elevation. His heart was lifted up because of his own beauty. His wisdom, once pure, became corrupted through self-admiration. He became intoxicated with his own splendor, and that inward exaltation became iniquity, the sin of pride.

> *"By the multitude of thy merchandise they have filled the midst of thee with violence, and thou hast sinned: therefore I will cast thee*

> *as profane out of the mountain of God: and I will destroy thee, O covering cherub, from the midst of the stones of fire.*
> *Thine heart was lifted up because of thy beauty, thou hast corrupted thy wisdom by reason of thy brightness: I will cast thee to the ground, I will lay thee before kings, that they may behold thee."*
> Ezekiel 28:16-17

Notice God's response. It was not simply a removal but a casting out, a forceful severing from the mountain of God, which prophetically symbolizes access to God's presence and voice. Pride disconnected Lucifer from proximity, from intimacy, and from the voice he once guarded.

> *"Thou hast defiled thy sanctuaries by the multitude of thine iniquities, by the iniquity of thy traffick..."*
> Ezekiel 28:18

Even his sanctuaries, the very places he was entrusted to protect, became defiled because of the iniquity of his trafficking. This trafficking speaks to the spreading of rebellion, the subtle turning of others' hearts through influence, charisma, and manipulation. Pride doesn't stay contained; it corrupts everything it touches.

God's judgment was swift and final:

> *"...Therefore will I bring forth a fire from the midst of thee, it shall devour thee, and I will bring thee to ashes upon the earth in the sight of all them that behold thee.*
> *All they that know thee among the people shall be astonished at thee: thou shalt be a terror, and never shalt thou be any more."*
> Ezekiel 28:18-19

FOUR // THE SIN THAT SILENCES GOD

The very light that once defined him became the fire that consumed him. He was brought to ashes in the sight of those who beheld him, becoming an eternal sign of what happens when created beings seek glory that belongs to God alone.

This is why pride is the only sin that disconnects creation from the voice of God. It exalts self above surrender, blinds the heart to correction, and makes one deaf to divine instruction. Where pride reigns, the voice of God is resisted, replaced, or outright rejected.

> *"Though the Lord be high, yet hath He respect unto the lowly: but the proud He knoweth afar off."*
> Psalm 138:6

This verse unveils a critical dimension of God's heart: His nearness to the humble and His distance from the proud. Though exalted above all, the Almighty bends low to dwell with the contrite, but pride repels His presence like darkness resists the light.

God hates pride because it is an active attempt to replace Him. It is the spirit of anti-dependence; the delusion that one can exist, function, or thrive apart from the Source of all life. Every created thing draws its breath, purpose, and sustenance from God. In Him, all things live, move, and have their being.

> *For in Him we live, and move, and have our being; as certain also of your own poets have said, For we are also His offspring."*
> Acts 17:28

Pride is a spiritual cancer; it is subtle, invasive, and deadly. Just as no wise physician will allow a cancer to remain unchecked in the body, God does not permit pride to dwell within His presence. Pride must be cut off because, like cancer, it cannot exist without a host. It seeks to attach itself to what is living in order to corrupt, consume, and ultimately destroy.

Therefore, the moment anyone engages in pride, whether in thought, posture, or motive, they are choosing to separate themselves from both the presence *and* the voice of God. God does not turn from them, but it is they who turn from Him. Pride lifts the soul high, and in doing so, it drifts far from the sound of Heaven. It is not the sin of the hands that causes this distance; it is the exaltation of the heart.

King Saul was a man both loved and anointed by God. He was chosen, empowered, and positioned for greatness. Yet he failed to honor God because of one fatal flaw: pride. When the Lord gave him a clear and simple instruction through the Prophet Samuel, his spiritual father, mentor, and divine guide, Saul chose partial obedience over full surrender.

God granted Saul many victories. He was given opportunity, authority, and favor, but in a single moment, pride exposed his heart. Instead of obeying the voice of the Lord, he leaned on his own understanding, seeking the approval of people over the pleasure of God. Just like Lucifer, Saul was *lifted in position but fallen in heart*, and it cost him everything.

Because of pride, Saul lost his place in God's grand plan for Israel. The Lord, who is never without a vessel, found Himself another king, not in a palace, but among the cattle. David, a boy forgotten by his own father and dismissed by his brothers, was beloved by God for one reason: his humility.

This is a sobering truth: no one is irreplaceable in the eyes of God. The Lord does not depend on vessels, He prepares them. He can raise up anyone at any moment, from any background, for any purpose. The only qualification He seeks is a heart postured in humility.

For it is not gifting that secures one's place in the kingdom, it is surrender. Pride, no matter how anointed it appears, always leads to replacement. Let's look at 1 Samuel 15.

FOUR // THE SIN THAT SILENCES GOD

1   *Samuel also said unto Saul, The Lord sent me to anoint thee to be king over his people, over Israel: now therefore hearken thou unto the voice of the words of the Lord.*
2   *Thus saith the Lord of hosts, I remember that which Amalek did to Israel, how he laid wait for him in the way, when he came up from Egypt.*
3   *Now go and smite Amalek, and utterly destroy all that they have, and spare them not; but slay both man and woman, infant and suckling, ox and sheep, camel and ass.*
4   *And Saul gathered the people together, and numbered them in Telaim, two hundred thousand footmen, and ten thousand men of Judah.*
5   *And Saul came to a city of Amalek, and laid wait in the valley.*
6   *And Saul said unto the Kenites, Go, depart, get you down from among the Amalekites, lest I destroy you with them: for ye shewed kindness to all the children of Israel, when they came up out of Egypt. So the Kenites departed from among the Amalekites.*
7   *And Saul smote the Amalekites from Havilah until thou comest to Shur, that is over against Egypt.*
8   *And he took Agag the king of the Amalekites alive, and utterly destroyed all the people with the edge of the sword.*
9   *But Saul and the people spared Agag, and the best of the sheep, and of the oxen, and of the fatlings, and the lambs, and all that was good, and would not utterly destroy them: but every thing that was vile and refuse, that they destroyed utterly.*
10   *Then came the word of the Lord unto Samuel, saying,*
11   *It repenteth me that I have set up Saul to be king: for he is turned back from following Me, and hath not performed My commandments. And it grieved Samuel; and he cried unto the Lord all night.*
12   *And when Samuel rose early to meet Saul in the morning, it*

was told Samuel, saying, Saul came to Carmel, and, behold, he set him up a place, and is gone about, and passed on, and gone down to Gilgal.

13 And Samuel came to Saul: and Saul said unto him, Blessed be thou of the Lord: I have performed the commandment of the Lord.

14 And Samuel said, What meaneth then this bleating of the sheep in mine ears, and the lowing of the oxen which I hear?

15 And Saul said, They have brought them from the Amalekites: for the people spared the best of the sheep and of the oxen, to sacrifice unto the Lord thy God; and the rest we have utterly destroyed.

16 Then Samuel said unto Saul, Stay, and I will tell thee what the Lord hath said to me this night. And he said unto him, Say on.

17 And Samuel said, When thou wast little in thine own sight, wast thou not made the head of the tribes of Israel, and the Lord anointed thee king over Israel?

18 And the Lord sent thee on a journey, and said, Go and utterly destroy the sinners the Amalekites, and fight against them until they be consumed.

19 Wherefore then didst thou not obey the voice of the Lord, but didst fly upon the spoil, and didst evil in the sight of the Lord?

20 And Saul said unto Samuel, Yea, I have obeyed the voice of the Lord, and have gone the way which the Lord sent me, and have brought Agag the king of Amalek, and have utterly destroyed the Amalekites.

21 But the people took of the spoil, sheep and oxen, the chief of the things which should have been utterly destroyed, to sacrifice unto the Lord thy God in Gilgal.

22 And Samuel said, Hath the Lord as great delight in burnt offerings and sacrifices, as in obeying the voice of the Lord? Behold,

FOUR // THE SIN THAT SILENCES GOD

to obey is better than sacrifice, and to hearken than the fat of rams.
23 For rebellion is as the sin of witchcraft, and stubbornness is as iniquity and idolatry. Because thou hast rejected the word of the Lord, he hath also rejected thee from being king.
24 And Saul said unto Samuel, I have sinned: for I have transgressed the commandment of the Lord, and thy words: because I feared the people, and obeyed their voice.
25 Now therefore, I pray thee, pardon my sin, and turn again with me, that I may worship the Lord.
26 And Samuel said unto Saul, I will not return with thee: for thou hast rejected the word of the Lord, and the Lord hath rejected thee from being king over Israel.
27 And as Samuel turned about to go away, he laid hold upon the skirt of his mantle, and it rent.
28 And Samuel said unto him, The Lord hath rent the kingdom of Israel from thee this day, and hath given it to a neighbour of thine, that is better than thou.
29 And also the Strength of Israel will not lie nor repent: for he is not a man, that he should repent.
30 Then he said, I have sinned: yet honour me now, I pray thee, before the elders of my people, and before Israel, and turn again with me, that I may worship the Lord thy God.
31 So Samuel turned again after Saul; and Saul worshipped the Lord.
1 Samuel 15:1-31

In this chapter, we witness the unraveling of a king not because of outward failure, but because of inward rebellion. Saul's downfall did not begin with disobedience; it began with pride that slowly hardened into stubbornness and ended in spiritual rejection.

The Lord, through Samuel the Prophet, gave Saul a clear and uncompromising instruction: *utterly destroy Amalek*. This was not a suggestion, but a divine decree rooted in justice and remembrance. Yet Saul obeyed selectively; he spared what seemed desirable and justified it under the guise of sacrifice. He preserved the things God had marked for destruction, and in doing so, he revealed the condition of his heart: a man who feared the people more than he feared God.

When Samuel confronts Saul, the king greets him with hollow religion: *"I have performed the commandment of the Lord."* But Samuel, discerning the truth, asks a haunting question: *"What meaneth then this bleating of the sheep...?"* In other words, if you truly obeyed, why do I hear what should have been silenced?

Partial obedience is still disobedience. And disobedience, especially when wrapped in religious justification, becomes rebellion. As Samuel declares by the Spirit: *"Rebellion is as the sin of witchcraft, and stubbornness is as iniquity and idolatry."* These are not light words. God equates resistance to His voice with the same spiritual darkness that governs sorcery and idolatry.

Saul's fall reveals a deeper truth: God values obedience over performance. He is not impressed by sacrifices that emerge from disobedient hearts. What He seeks is not ritual, but reverence. Not offerings, but obedience.

And then Samuel delivers the judgment that would echo through the pages of history: *"Because you have rejected the word of the Lord, He has also rejected you from being king."* Even Saul's confession is telling. He admits his sin, but immediately seeks honor before the people. *"Yet honor me now... before the elders..."* His concern was not restoration with God but reputation before men. He wanted to worship, but without true repentance. He wanted appearance over authenticity.

Thus, the kingdom was torn from him, not just symbolically, but literally, as Saul grasped the prophet's robe and it ripped in his hand. Samuel, under divine unction, declared: *"The Lord hath rent the kingdom of Israel from thee this day, and given it to a neighbor... better than thou."*

FOUR // THE SIN THAT SILENCES GOD

This chapter reveals that:

- Pride resists instruction, even when it comes from a trusted voice.
- Fear of man is a doorway to rebellion.
- God does not overlook disobedience simply because we offer worship.
- Humility secures favor, but pride invites replacement.

Saul's story is a solemn reminder: being chosen is not enough. It is obedience that sustains the calling. In the end, it is better to walk in quiet humility than to reign in prideful disobedience.

Five
PROPHETIC PRAYERS

FIVE // PROPHETIC PRAYERS

Prayer is one of the most misunderstood tools that God has granted to the body of Christ. If we truly understood prayer and how God intended for us to use it within the prophetic, many who reject the prophetic would come to believe in it. Prayer is indeed a divine tool ordained by God. Yet, if we look to Scripture, from the very beginning of man's creation, we'll see something profound: the art of prayer was not originally necessary. Adam did not pray while he was in the garden because he walked in perfect communion with God. There was no veil, no hindrance separating man from his Creator.

> *"And they heard the voice of the LORD God walking in the garden in the cool of the day: and Adam and his wife hid themselves from the presence of the LORD God amongst the trees of the garden."*
> Genesis 3:8

Notice this: Adam and his wife did not need to pray for God's presence to descend. They lived in His presence; it was the atmosphere they breathed, their daily reality. This is the communion that the Lord Jesus came to restore. Prayer was never meant to be eternal; communion was. Prayer was always meant to be a tool, not the end itself. Right now, even in Heaven there is prayer, as beings such as angels and saints intercede for those on earth. When the earth is made new, however, and all is restored to perfection, prayer will cease. Worship, love, and communion will remain, but prayer, as we know it, will no longer be necessary.

PRAYER ELEVATES SPIRITUAL CONSCIOUSNESS

When man sinned, as I stated in an earlier chapter, he began to lose his spiritual senses and communion with the invisible world. Above all, we lost the ability to perceive God clearly, for we became bound by the flesh.

> *"And the eyes of them both were opened, and they knew that they were naked; and they sewed fig leaves together, and made themselves aprons."*
> Genesis 3:7

This was not the opening of spiritual eyes, but the awakening of fleshly awareness. Their spiritual sight dimmed, and carnal perception took its place. What was once a life led by the spirit was now dominated by the senses of the flesh. They could no longer see God; they could only see themselves.

The moment Adam and Eve's eyes were opened to the natural, they became blind to the spiritual. They were no longer aware of the God who walked with them; instead, they were aware of their nakedness, their shame, and their separation. The flesh became their new lens, and fear became their first reaction.

> *"And they heard the voice of the LORD God walking in the garden in the cool of the day: and Adam and his wife hid themselves from the presence of the LORD God amongst the trees of the garden."*
> Genesis 3:8

Notice how man, who once ran to God, now hid from Him. This is what happens when spiritual consciousness is lost: God's voice becomes frightening instead of familiar.

Prophetic prayer is the divine antidote to this condition. Every time we engage in true prayer, we are not just speaking into the air; we are tuning the frequency of our spirit back to Heaven. We are reorienting ourselves toward the invisible realm where God dwells. This is why those who live a life of prophetic prayer begin to experience visions, divine impressions, angelic encounters, and heightened sensitivity to the Holy Spirit. Their spirits are no longer suffocated by the flesh but quickened by communion.

Prophetic prayer does not ask for things, it seeks communion. It lifts the soul out of the mud of earthly distraction and sets the eyes of the spirit back on the throne of God. This is why Paul said:

> *"Set your affection on things above, not on things on the earth."*
> Colossians 3:2

Without prayer, the soul sinks. With prayer, the soul and spirit soar.

PRAYER PROVOKES HEAVEN TO OPEN

> *"Now when all the people were baptized, it came to pass, that Jesus also being baptized, and praying, the heaven was opened."*
> Luke 3:21

Prophetic prayer provokes an open Heaven. This means the will of God is no longer restricted to the unseen realm; it is invited to invade the earth. While our Lord Jesus was being baptized, Heaven did not open merely because He was the Son of God. The scripture is clear: He was baptized, and praying, and *then* the heavens opened. It was the union of obedience and prophetic intercession that activated the realm above.

This is why we are instructed to pray before doing anything. Prayer positions us beneath an open Heaven. Without it, we may carry out divine assignments under closed skies, with limited visibility and restricted flow. But when we pray, we provoke divine activity; we call down rain, revelation, and release. Elijah understood this.

> *"Elias was a man subject to like passions as we are, and he prayed earnestly that it might not rain: and it rained not on the earth by the space of three years and six months.*
> *And he prayed again, and the heaven gave rain, and the earth brought forth her fruit."*
> James 5:17-18

He prayed, and the heavens withheld. He prayed again, and they poured out. Without prayer, there is no access to the heavenly realm. Prayer is not just communication; it is a key. It unlocks the invisible. It gives man legal right to pull the reality of Heaven into the realm of earth. Prophetic prayer does not beg for visitation, it provokes it. It does not ask God to show up; it creates a landing place for His glory.

PRAYER INVITES ANGELIC VISITATION

When Adam and Eve were in the garden, they lived in perfect harmony with both God and His angelic hosts. They knew no life separated from divine presence. One of the names of God is *The LORD of Hosts*, meaning, *the God of Heaven's Armies*. This name reveals a truth that cannot be ignored: wherever God is, there will be angels.

Angelic beings are drawn to atmospheres that reflect Heaven. Prophetic prayer is one of the primary ways we recreate those atmospheres on earth.

> *"And He saith unto him, Verily, verily, I say unto you, Hereafter ye shall see heaven open, and the angels of God ascending and descending upon the Son of man."*
> John 1:51

When Jesus said this to Nathanael, He was not merely making a poetic statement. He was revealing a spiritual reality: His atmosphere commanded angels. Wherever He walked, angelic beings were moving, ascending and descending on assignment as Heaven responded to the rhythm of His Spirit. This is what we were meant to walk in, the dimension of divine partnership. It is where angelic assistance is not the exception but the norm for the believer, especially for those walking prophetically.

Consider Jacob. The first time he encountered angels, it was accidental. He was running for his life, alone and afraid, and unknowingly stumbled upon a realm he had never accessed before:

> *"And he dreamed, and behold a ladder set up on the earth, and the top of it reached to heaven: and behold the angels of God ascending and descending on it.*
> *And, behold, the LORD stood above it, and said, I am the LORD God of Abraham thy father, and the God of Isaac: the land whereon thou liest, to thee will I give it, and to thy seed;*
> *And thy seed shall be as the dust of the earth, and thou shalt spread abroad to the west, and to the east, and to the north, and to the south: and in thee and in thy seed shall all the families of the earth be blessed.*

And, behold, I am with thee, and will keep thee in all places whither thou goest, and will bring thee again into this land; for I will not leave thee, until I have done that which I have spoken to thee of.
And Jacob awaked out of his sleep, and he said, Surely the LORD is in this place; and I knew it not.
And he was afraid, and said, How dreadful is this place! this is none other but the house of God, and this is the gate of heaven."
Genesis 28:12-17

Jacob was shocked. He did not realize he had laid his head upon a portal, a spiritual gateway. The ladder he saw was a prophetic image of angelic traffic between Heaven and Earth; but that was only the beginning. Years later, Jacob matured. He no longer waited for chance encounters. He now understood that the supernatural could be pursued. And so, he deliberately positioned himself to encounter the angelic again:

"And Jacob was left alone; and there wrestled a man with him until the breaking of the day.
And when he saw that he prevailed not against him, he touched the hollow of his thigh; and the hollow of Jacob's thigh was out of joint, as he wrestled with him.
And he said, Let me go, for the day breaketh. And he said, I will not let thee go, except thou bless me."
Genesis 32:24-26

This was no dream. Jacob physically wrestled with an angel, face to face. What began as a dream in Bethel became a divine confrontation at Peniel. This is the power of sustained, prophetic prayer; it matures us from experiencers into engagers.

Cornelius, a Roman centurion, provides another key revelation.

FIVE // PROPHETIC PRAYERS

Though he was not yet fully a part of the covenant people of Israel, his hunger for God provoked something divine. Through fasting, giving, and constant prayer, he attracted the attention of Heaven:

> *"He saw in a vision evidently about the ninth hour of the day an angel of God coming in to him, and saying unto him, Cornelius. And when he looked on him, he was afraid, and said, What is it, Lord? And he said unto him, Thy prayers and thine alms are come up for a memorial before God."*
> Acts 10:3-4

Cornelius was not only noticed, but he was remembered. His prayers and almsgiving had risen before God as a memorial. The result? An angel was dispatched with instructions that led to the salvation of his entire household.

Then consider Peter, imprisoned for preaching the gospel. The early church didn't panic; they prayed. But it wasn't ordinary prayer; it was continual, fervent intercession. The result?

> *"Peter therefore was kept in prison: but prayer was made without ceasing of the church unto God for him.*
> *And when Herod would have brought him forth, the same night Peter was sleeping between two soldiers, bound with two chains: and the keepers before the door kept the prison.*
> *And, behold, the angel of the Lord came upon him, and a light shined in the prison: and he smote Peter on the side, and raised him up, saying, Arise up quickly. And his chains fell off from his hands."*
> Acts 12:5-7

The angel of the Lord did not appear *before* they prayed; he came *because* they prayed. The saints didn't need to break open the prison; their prayers opened Heaven, and Heaven sent an angel to break open the prison.

We must also remember Daniel, a man of deep intercession and fasting. His consistent discipline in prayer brought him face to face with the angel Gabriel, not once, but multiple times:

> *"Yea, whiles I was speaking in prayer, even the man Gabriel, whom I had seen in the vision at the beginning, being caused to fly swiftly, touched me about the time of the evening oblation.*
> *And he informed me, and talked with me, and said, O Daniel, I am now come forth to give thee skill and understanding."*
> Daniel 9:21-22

Again, in chapter 10, Daniel fasted and prayed for 21 days until the same angel came again. This time he was delayed by demonic resistance, but Daniel's perseverance in the spirit brought about breakthrough.

> *"Then said he unto me, Fear not, Daniel: for from the first day that thou didst set thine heart to understand, and to chasten thyself before thy God, thy words were heard, and I am come for thy words. But the prince of the kingdom of Persia withstood me one and twenty days: but, lo, Michael, one of the chief princes, came to help me; and I remained there with the kings of Persia."*
> Daniel 10:12-13

Prophetic prayer gives angels permission to move. It creates legal grounds for Heaven's messengers to engage in earthly affairs.

> *"Are they not all ministering spirits, sent forth to minister for them who shall be heirs of salvation?"*
> Hebrews 1:14

FIVE // PROPHETIC PRAYERS

Though he was not yet fully a part of the covenant people of Israel, his hunger for God provoked something divine. Through fasting, giving, and constant prayer, he attracted the attention of Heaven:

> *"He saw in a vision evidently about the ninth hour of the day an angel of God coming in to him, and saying unto him, Cornelius. And when he looked on him, he was afraid, and said, What is it, Lord? And he said unto him, Thy prayers and thine alms are come up for a memorial before God."*
> Acts 10:3-4

Cornelius was not only noticed, but he was remembered. His prayers and almsgiving had risen before God as a memorial. The result? An angel was dispatched with instructions that led to the salvation of his entire household.

Then consider Peter, imprisoned for preaching the gospel. The early church didn't panic; they prayed. But it wasn't ordinary prayer; it was continual, fervent intercession. The result?

> *"Peter therefore was kept in prison: but prayer was made without ceasing of the church unto God for him.*
> *And when Herod would have brought him forth, the same night Peter was sleeping between two soldiers, bound with two chains: and the keepers before the door kept the prison.*
> *And, behold, the angel of the Lord came upon him, and a light shined in the prison: and he smote Peter on the side, and raised him up, saying, Arise up quickly. And his chains fell off from his hands."*
> Acts 12:5-7

The angel of the Lord did not appear *before* they prayed; he came *because* they prayed. The saints didn't need to break open the prison; their prayers opened Heaven, and Heaven sent an angel to break open the prison.

We must also remember Daniel, a man of deep intercession and fasting. His consistent discipline in prayer brought him face to face with the angel Gabriel, not once, but multiple times:

> *"Yea, whiles I was speaking in prayer, even the man Gabriel, whom I had seen in the vision at the beginning, being caused to fly swiftly, touched me about the time of the evening oblation. And he informed me, and talked with me, and said, O Daniel, I am now come forth to give thee skill and understanding."*
> Daniel 9:21-22

Again, in chapter 10, Daniel fasted and prayed for 21 days until the same angel came again. This time he was delayed by demonic resistance, but Daniel's perseverance in the spirit brought about breakthrough.

> *"Then said he unto me, Fear not, Daniel: for from the first day that thou didst set thine heart to understand, and to chasten thyself before thy God, thy words were heard, and I am come for thy words. But the prince of the kingdom of Persia withstood me one and twenty days: but, lo, Michael, one of the chief princes, came to help me; and I remained there with the kings of Persia."*
> Daniel 10:12-13

Prophetic prayer gives angels permission to move. It creates legal grounds for Heaven's messengers to engage in earthly affairs.

> *"Are they not all ministering spirits, sent forth to minister for them who shall be heirs of salvation?"*
> Hebrews 1:14

FIVE // PROPHETIC PRAYERS

The Church needs angels, and prophets especially need angelic help. Throughout scripture, prophets never operated independently of angels. From Elijah being fed by one, to Zechariah receiving visions from one, and even John receiving the entire book of Revelation through one, it is evident that angelic assistance is vital.

Prophetic prayer provokes this dimension. It is the meeting place between earth and Heaven, between the natural and the supernatural. It's where portals open, revelation flows, deliverance is dispatched, and angelic assignments are released. If your ministry is absent of angelic partnership, you must examine your prayer life. Where there is prophetic intercession, there will be divine visitation.

PRAYER SUSTAINS POWER

There is a quote I often heard growing up in Nairobi, Kenya, something many pastors would declare with conviction: *"A prayerless Christian is a powerless Christian."* This quote is true, yet it needs a deeper revelation.

Prayer is not just important for the believer; it is absolutely essential, especially for those called into the prophetic. Prayer is the lifeline of the Christian. I will say it again: prayer is more important than oxygen. Without oxygen, the body dies; without prayer, the spirit suffocates and collapses under the pressures of life and destiny.

Now hear me clearly: prayer by itself is not powerful. All religions pray, and most of them even fast. True power, however, is released only when prayer is directed correctly to El Olam, the Everlasting God, the Father of our Lord Jesus Christ. Prayer is powerful not because of the act itself, but because of *who* you are praying to and *how* you are positioned before Him.

Prayer is Heaven's legal channel to earth. Prayer is the divine transaction point where weakness is exchanged for strength, confusion for wisdom, human limitation for supernatural ability. The Scriptures declare:

> "...The effectual fervent prayer of a righteous man availeth much."
> James 5:16

Prayer is where power is imparted, authority is established, and destiny is fortified. Without prayer, there is no sustained power.

THE EVERLASTING POWER SOURCE

> "Hast thou not known? hast thou not heard, that the everlasting God, the LORD, the Creator of the ends of the earth, fainteth not, neither is weary? there is no searching of His understanding.
> He giveth power to the faint; and to them that have no might He increaseth strength.
> Even the youths shall faint and be weary, and the young men shall utterly fall:
> But they that wait upon the LORD shall renew their strength; they shall mount up with wings as eagles; they shall run, and not be weary; and they shall walk, and not faint."
> Isaiah 40:28-31

When you pray, you engage with El Olam, the God of eternity, who never faints, never weakens, and never needs rest. You are not praying to a tired deity. You are praying to the *Borei*, the Creator, the One who spoke galaxies into existence and whose strength has no end.

FIVE // PROPHETIC PRAYERS

In prayer, you plug your spirit into the eternal battery of divine might.

> *"There is no searching of His understanding."*

God's understanding (Hebrew: *tevunah*) is vast, infinite, and beyond human comprehension. Through prayer, you gain access to divine secrets, heavenly strategies, and mysteries that the mind of man could never uncover without revelation.

PRAYER DOWNLOADS THE MIND OF GOD INTO THE SPIRIT OF MAN

> *"He giveth power to the faint; and to them that have no might he increaseth strength."*

Those who come faint (Hebrew: *ya'ef*) are met with *koach*, divine force and strength. In prayer, God does not just comfort you, He imparts power. When you come to Him empty, He fills you. When you come weary, He infuses you with the might of Heaven. Prayer is the divine exchange point:

> Your exhaustion for His energy.
> Your weakness for His power.
> Your despair for His dominion.

> *"Even the youths shall faint and be weary, and the young men shall utterly fall…"*

Natural strength, no matter how youthful or vibrant, will

eventually collapse. Your gifting alone will fail you. Your zeal alone will run out. Without prayer, even the strongest will fall. Prayerlessness is dangerous because it leaves even the anointed exposed. Prayer sustains what God begins.

> *"But they that wait upon the Lord shall renew their strength..."*

Those who wait (*qavah*), who bind themselves tightly to the Lord in prayer, shall *chalaph*, be renewed, transformed, exchanged.

Prayer does not simply recharge you; it transforms you. It replaces the old man with the new, the human strength with divine empowerment. In prayer, your identity changes. In prayer, your capacity expands. In prayer, you become a vessel capable of carrying glory.

> *"They shall mount up with wings as eagles..."*

In prayer, you *alah*; you ascend. You rise above warfare. You rise above accusations. You rise above earthly systems. You move in the currents of the Spirit and operate from heavenly altitude.

PRAYER GRANTS THE EAGLE'S VISION AND THE EAGLE'S ELEVATION.

> *"They shall run, and not be weary; and they shall walk, and not faint."*

Prayer imparts endurance for the long race and strength for the slow journey. When you are running toward destiny, prayer ensures you do not collapse under pressure. When you are walking through valleys, prayer ensures you do not faint from discouragement. Whether soaring, running, or walking, prayer sustains you.

A PROPHETIC CHARGE

Prayer is not a religious routine. Prayer is the fountain of supernatural power. It is the force that binds the believer to the Source of all strength. It is the heavenly highway where divine reinforcements are released. It is the secret to maintaining prophetic sight, sustaining authority, and finishing your race with joy.

A prayerless Christian is truly a powerless Christian; but a praying believer is an unstoppable force in the earth. Return to prayer. Guard your altar. Keep the flame burning, and you will soar where others fall, you will endure where others faint, and you will prevail where others perish.

"Men ought always to pray, and not to faint."
Luke 18:1

Six
PROPHETS FROM THE WOMB

SIX // PROPHETS FROM THE WOMB

UNLOCKING THE SECRETS OF INHERITANCE AND SPIRITUAL TRANSFER

> *"For I long to see you, that I may impart unto you some spiritual gift, to the end ye may be established."*
> Romans 1:11

Spiritual gifts are given by God in a variety of ways. They are not earned; they are distributed by grace, purpose, and calling. Some are born with gifts, some receive them by impartation, and others are granted spiritual gifts following the baptism of the Holy Spirit after salvation.

What is often overlooked is this divine reality: some men and women of God have had the Spirit of God resting upon them from birth. This is not common, but it is biblical. The Scriptures give us examples of individuals who were marked by the Spirit while still in the womb, and chosen before the world ever knew their name.

Let us examine some key figures.

JOHN THE BAPTIST

> *"And there appeared unto him an angel of the Lord standing on the right side of the altar of incense.*
> *And when Zacharias saw him, he was troubled, and fear fell upon him.*
> *But the angel said unto him, Fear not, Zacharias: for thy prayer is heard; and thy wife Elisabeth shall bear thee a son, and thou shalt call his name John.*

And thou shalt have joy and gladness; and many shall rejoice at his birth.
For he shall be great in the sight of the Lord, and shall drink neither wine nor strong drink; and he shall be filled with the Holy Ghost, even from his mother's womb."
Luke 1:11-15

Before John was born, his mission was already sealed. The angel of the Lord declared that John would be great in the sight of God, and that he would be filled with the Holy Ghost even before birth. His consecration was not a choice he made later in life but a divine ordination from the womb.

PROPHET ISAIAH

"Listen, O isles, unto me; and hearken, ye people, from afar; the LORD hath called me from the womb; from the bowels of my mother hath He made mention of my name."
Isaiah 49:1

Isaiah's prophetic destiny was not discovered in adulthood; it was embedded in his being from the womb. He was called, named, and set apart before his first breath. God had already branded him with purpose in his mother's body.

PROPHET JEREMIAH

"Before I formed thee in the belly I knew thee; and before thou camest forth out of the womb I sanctified thee, and I ordained thee a prophet unto the nations."
Jeremiah 1:5

SIX // PROPHETS FROM THE WOMB

This scripture is perhaps the clearest proof of pre-birth ordination. Jeremiah was not just known; he was sanctified and ordained before he ever cried out as an infant. His office was not a result of ministry school or a supernatural encounter later in life; it was God's sovereign decision.

KING DAVID

"I was cast upon thee from the womb: thou art my God from my mother's belly."
Psalm 22:10

Though the Scriptures do not state explicitly that David was filled with the Holy Spirit from the womb, his language and spiritual insight suggest a deep, early awareness of God. We see him operating prophetically and writing psalms while still in isolation; he was tending sheep, yet discerning heaven. His understanding far surpassed his peers, suggesting a life formed early by God's presence.

Now contrast this with King Saul:

"And the Spirit of the LORD will come upon thee, and thou shalt prophesy with them, and shalt be turned into another man."
1 Samuel 10:6

"And when they came thither to the hill, behold, a company of prophets met him; and the Spirit of God came upon him, and he prophesied among them.
And it came to pass, when all that knew him beforetime saw that, behold, he prophesied among the prophets, then the people said one to another, What is this that is come unto the son of Kish? Is Saul also among the prophets?"
1 Samuel 10:10-11

Saul *received* the Holy Spirit later in life. He was not born with it, and we see that his prophetic activity was temporary and circumstantial. He was *transformed* by the Spirit, but not *formed* by the Spirit from birth, as David appeared to be. The contrast is clear: David carried something innate, Saul received something external.

SAMSON: THE NAZARITE FROM THE WOMB

"And the angel of the LORD appeared unto the woman, and said unto her, Behold now, thou art barren, and bearest not: but thou shalt conceive, and bear a son.
Now therefore beware, I pray thee, and drink not wine nor strong drink, and eat not any unclean thing:
For, lo, thou shalt conceive, and bear a son; and no razor shall come on his head: for the child shall be a Nazarite unto God from the womb: and he shall begin to deliver Israel out of the hand of the Philistines."
Judges 13:3-5

Samson was set apart before his birth, consecrated to God through a vow he didn't choose, but which governed his life. Though the text doesn't say he was filled with the Holy Spirit from the womb, we see that the Spirit of the Lord would come upon him with power, enabling him to accomplish feats no man could explain.

His hair was the symbol of his covenant, but the source of his strength was the Spirit of God. What's profound is this: even in moral failure, God would still move to fulfill His purpose through Samson. A Nazarite from the womb, Samson's strength flowed from consecration, not personal merit. His consecration provided access to the Spirit even in flawed moments, because it was not built on performance; it was based on divine calling from birth.

SIX // PROPHETS FROM THE WOMB

A PROPHET FROM THE WOMB: MY CALLING AND ENCOUNTER WITH THE LORD JESUS CHRIST

By divine grace, I have loved the Lord Jesus Christ before anyone preached Him to me. Before I understood salvation, before I knew what sin was, or had ever heard of the Holy Spirit, I was drawn to Him. His presence called out to me, and something deep in my spirit responded, even as a child.

Then came the night that marked me forever. It was the year 1992, in Nairobi, Kenya, in a community called South C, inside a neighborhood named Mogadishu, after the capital city of Somalia. I was very sick with malaria, and my condition was worsening. There was no relief, no sign of recovery. But in that dark night of affliction, light broke through.

The Lord Jesus Christ appeared to me. He stood before me, not as a story, not as a sermon, but as the Living God. His presence filled the room and every part of my being. His voice was powerful, yet full of mercy. He looked at me and spoke words that changed the course of my life:

> *"I have chosen you and appointed you a prophet. I will send you to another nation, far from where you are now, and there, I will bring people from all over the world to hear you speak. Through you, I will show great signs, miracles, and wonders, so that they may know I have sent you. Many will come to repentance and salvation, and the powers of darkness will be put to shame."*

From that moment, He assigned an angel to my life who has never left me since. From that hour, my eyes were opened. I began to see visions. I could prophesy with clarity. Divine understanding flooded my mind like a river. Revelation and insight began to flow through me, though I was still just a child. I had never read a book on the prophetic. No one had laid hands on me. This was Jesus Christ Himself, coming to awaken what He had placed inside me from the foundation of the world.

Even my family was left in awe. They were puzzled: how could one of their own become a prophet? But the seal of God was undeniable.

With this divine calling came a holy consecration. The Lord warned me that I must never touch alcohol or any form of drugs. To this day, by His grace, I have never tasted alcohol, never touched drugs, and never violated the foods He told me not to eat. I have lived with that sacred restriction my entire life, not out of fear, but out of honor. Because when you've seen the Lord, and when you've heard His voice, nothing in this world is worth disobedience.

This is my story. I didn't choose the prophetic, the prophetic chose me. Before man recognized me, God called me. Before I was mentored, I was visited. Before I was trained, I was touched. Every miracle, every revelation, every soul that comes to Jesus through the ministry that He gave me, is all rooted in the night that the Lord Himself stepped into a small room in Nairobi and called me by name.

I am a prophet by birth, by encounter, and by divine assignment, living only to fulfill the will of the One who called me.

CARRIERS OF PRE-BIRTH PURPOSE

When we speak of spiritual gifts and anointing, we must understand that God is a God of patterns. He still raises prophets, deliverers, and voices across generations, yet He does not raise them all in the same way. Some are awakened through encounters, while others are trained through trials. Still, there are others, such as John, Jeremiah, Isaiah, David, and Samson, who are born with fire in their bones and oil on their heads. These individuals don't become anointed: they discover the anointing already within. Their lives unfold like scrolls already written.

As it was then, so it still is today. There are those walking the earth who were called from the womb, whose spirits were touched before their minds were formed. They may not fit traditional molds. They may rise outside of systems. But the seal of God is upon them. These are not ordinary men, they are ordained ones; and when they yield in humility and submission to divine process, they shake nations.

Seven
IMPARTATION AND MENTORSHIP

SEVEN // IMPARTATION AND MENTORSHIP

HEAVEN'S HIDDEN SYSTEM

Everyone who walks in the prophetic, or desires to, must come to a crucial realization: the kind of mentor you are submitted to determines the level of prophetic expression you will walk in. Your impartation is directly tied to your posture, your perception, and your alignment with the one God has placed over you.

Many in the body of Christ struggle to grow in the prophetic, not because they lack desire or hunger, but because they misunderstand the system of impartation. Impartation is not automatic. It is not absorbed casually. And it is not received by merely being around greatness. Impartation requires revelation.

If you don't understand who your mentor truly is, that is, their spiritual ranking, their office, their grace, and the inheritance they carry, you will never fully draw from the well within them. Elisha recognized Elijah as more than a teacher and more than a prophet: he saw him as, *"My father, my father, the chariot of Israel, and the horsemen thereof"* (2 Kings 2:12). That recognition unlocked the double portion.

Some people think that if they can just keep praying long enough, eventually God will give them the gift they desire. However, prayer alone does not grant impartation. If the gift did not come when the Holy Spirit first rested upon you, then what you seek may not come through your own efforts, but through someone who already walks in what you're desiring.

> *"For I long to see you, that I may impart unto you some spiritual gift, to the end ye may be established."*
> Romans 1:11

Impartation is scriptural, relational, and intentional.

THE POSTURE OF A TRUE SON

God often hides your next dimension in someone else. He wraps it in a mentor, a prophet, or a spiritual father, someone whose ceiling is meant to become your floor. However, you will not access it unless you come with the right posture: honor, humility, and hunger. You don't receive impartation by observation. You receive it by submission.

Submission is not passivity. Submission is active obedience, servanthood, and trust in the vessel God has chosen for your life. Being around a prophet doesn't mean you'll become prophetic, especially if you lack submission. Gehazi was around Elisha, but he inherited a curse, not a mantle. Why? Because his posture was wrong.

> *"But he went in, and stood before his master. And Elisha said unto him, Whence comest thou, Gehazi? And he said, Thy servant went no whither.*
> *And he said unto him, Went not mine heart with thee, when the man turned again from his chariot to meet thee? Is it a time to receive money, and to receive garments, and oliveyards, and vineyards, and sheep, and oxen, and menservants, and maidservants?*
> *The leprosy therefore of Naaman shall cleave unto thee, and unto thy seed for ever. And he went out from his presence a leper as white as snow."*
> 2 Kings 5:25-27

On the other hand, Elisha served Elijah faithfully, and what Elijah carried was multiplied in him. Elisha cried out, "My father, my father," and then the mantle fell.

> *"And it came to pass, when they were gone over, that Elijah said*

SEVEN // IMPARTATION AND MENTORSHIP

> *unto Elisha, Ask what I shall do for thee, before I be taken away from thee. And Elisha said, I pray thee, let a double portion of thy spirit be upon me.*
> *And he said, Thou hast asked a hard thing: nevertheless, if thou see me when I am taken from thee, it shall be so unto thee; but if not, it shall not be so.*
> *And it came to pass, as they still went on, and talked, that, behold, there appeared a chariot of fire, and horses of fire, and parted them both asunder; and Elijah went up by a whirlwind into heaven.*
> *And Elisha saw it, and he cried, My father, my father, the chariot of Israel, and the horsemen thereof. And he saw him no more: and he took hold of his own clothes, and rent them in two pieces.*
> *He took up also the mantle of Elijah that fell from him, and went back, and stood by the bank of Jordan."*
> 2 Kings 2:9-13

You don't inherit what you admire; you inherit what you serve. If you want to walk in prophetic power, accuracy, and revelation, you must do more than pray. You must discern who carries what you need, and you must align with honor. Why? Because God is not obligated to give you what He already placed in someone else if you refuse to receive it through them.

A CHARGE TO THE EMERGING PROPHETIC GENERATION

Hear me by the Spirit of God: The prophetic is not just about what you can see, say, or declare. It is about how you submit, how you serve, and how you honor. True authority in the Spirit does not come from charisma; it comes from covenant. It does not reside with a platform, but with the people and the prophets God has chosen for your destiny. If you're called to the prophetic, ask yourself:

- Who am I submitted to?
- Have I discerned the one God assigned to pour into me?
- Do I serve with joy, or with hidden expectations?
- Am I entitled, or entrusted?

If your answer is built on humility, the path before you will be bright. If pride or ambition have taken root, they will delay your rising, or destroy it altogether. May you be a generation that seeks not just power, but alignment. Not just vision, but voice under covering. Not just gifting, but grace to steward it well. In this kingdom, inheritance is not claimed by gift, it is claimed by honor; and honor always leads to impartation.

Eight
THE LAWS OF IMPARTATION

EIGHT // THE LAWS OF IMPARTATION

Throughout generations, the Lord God has graced nations with extraordinary gifts, namely men and women whom Heaven trusted with profound revelation, healing virtue, and prophetic fire. These individuals were not ordinary; they were divine deposits sent to shift atmospheres, shape destinies, and awaken nations. Unfortunately, despite their presence and power, many believers missed their moment.

God, in His mercy, does not raise generals for show. God raises generals for distribution. Every true vessel carries not only a message, but a mantle. Those mantles are not meant to die with them; they are meant to be transferred, multiplied, and continued. Sadly, much of the Body of Christ has not understood the laws of impartation. As a result, many callings remain unactivated, many gifts lie dormant, and many destinies have been delayed or derailed.

MISSED INHERITANCES: A TRAGIC PATTERN

Let us consider some of the towering figures in the history of the Church.

PROPHET WILLIAM MARRION BRANHAM

Born on April 6th, 1909, Prophet Branham was a born seer. His prophetic ministry officially launched on May 7th, 1946, marked by stunning accuracy, supernatural visions, and mighty healing miracles. He operated in both foretelling and forth-telling, and secrets of men's hearts were laid bare in his presence. Angels would visit him. Light would shine around him. God trusted him with deep prophetic mysteries.

Yet, despite all this, Prophet Branham died without any clear impartation or spiritual succession. No one in his circle, despite being around him, received the full replication of his spirit. Why? Not because the mantle was unavailable, but because the laws of impartation were not honored, taught, or pursued.

PROPHETESS MARIA WOODWORTH-ETTER

Known as the "Mother of Pentecost," she was born on July 22nd, 1844, and moved in signs, wonders, and waves of revival that would leave entire cities shaken under the power of God. Trances, healings, and visitations were common in her meetings. She was a pioneer and trailblazer for women in ministry before such a thing was ever accepted. She began ministering powerfully in 1918, leaving a visible mark in Pentecostal history.

Sadly, like Branham, she died without passing on her mantle. No one received a full impartation or direct continuation of the grace she carried. The well was deep, but no one drew from it.

WHY THIS MATTERS NOW

These powerful gifts, these spiritual blueprints, are missing in our time; not because God stopped giving them, but because previous generations failed to receive and sustain impartation. We are living in a time where many in the Church have been conditioned to believe that supernatural gifts are no longer for today; that they were confined to the Bible's dispensations. This blindness came because mantles were not passed and wells were not reopened.

"One generation shall praise Thy works to another, and shall

declare Thy mighty acts."
Psalm 145:4

When a generation fails to pass on the mantle, the next one forgets what is possible.

THE PRINCIPLE WE MUST RECOVER

Impartation is not automatic. It is not casual. It must be understood, honored, and pursued with hunger and humility.

"For I long to see you, that I may impart unto you some spiritual gift, to the end ye may be established."
Romans 1:11

Paul understood that spiritual stability and effectiveness often comes through impartation, not just information. You can sit under a prophet for years and never become prophetic if you don't understand how to posture yourself.

God is restoring this understanding in our time. He is raising up fathers, generals, and prophetic voices who are not only carriers but givers. They are those who walk in grace and know how to release it to the next generation.

If we don't recover the laws of impartation, we will keep watching mantles fall to the ground instead of falling upon sons, and we will keep losing what Heaven intended for us to inherit. But, if we align and posture ourselves in honor, service, and spiritual understanding, we will see what generations before us missed. Then, we will not only receive mantles, but we will multiply them.

A GENERATION THAT BELIEVES MORE IN DARKNESS THAN IN POWER

One of the tragic results of failing to understand and receive impartation is this: we now have a generation in the Church that believes more in demonic activity than in the power of the Holy Spirit. When they see true prophetic utterance, instead of discerning the presence of God, they assume manipulation, arrangement, or the operation of a familiar spirit.

Why? Because the previous generations did not preserve the purity and continuity of supernatural grace. They failed to receive or sustain impartation, and in doing so, they left a spiritual vacuum. Inevitably, where there is no demonstration of power, skepticism grows.

This is why prophetic accuracy is now questioned, not celebrated. When God speaks through His vessels, many believers cannot discern whether it is the Holy Spirit or something counterfeit. The spiritual senses of the Church have been dulled by absence, not deception. What they call false is sometimes simply unfamiliar, because they have never been taught to discern, never seen it demonstrated authentically, and never sat under a mantle where impartation flowed.

> *"But the natural man receiveth not the things of the Spirit of God: for they are foolishness unto him: neither can he know them, because they are spiritually discerned."*
> 1 Corinthians 2:14

We have more faith in demonic strategies than in divine solutions. We shout about curses more than covenants. We believe the devil can destroy, but struggle to believe God still delivers. This is what happens when mantles die without transfer.

EIGHT // THE LAWS OF IMPARTATION

Notwithstanding, in every generation, God reserves a remnant. In this generation, He is restoring the understanding of spiritual inheritance, impartation, and supernatural discernment, so that the Church may once again walk in power, not just in words.

THE LAWS OF IMPARTATION

1. THE LAW OF RECOGNITION

You cannot receive from what you do not recognize. Impartation begins with the ability to spiritually perceive who God has sent into your life. Many miss their moment of elevation because they reduce great vessels to common people. Jesus Himself was rejected in Nazareth because they saw Him as "Joseph's son," not the Christ.

"He that receiveth a prophet in the name of a prophet shall receive a prophet's reward; and he that receiveth a righteous man in the name of a righteous man shall receive a righteous man's reward."
Matthew 10:41

If you see a prophet only as a man, you receive a man's reward. But if you perceive the office and grace they carry, you open yourself to inheritance.

2. THE LAW OF PROXIMITY

Spiritual inheritance flows best in closeness. Elisha didn't just admire Elijah; he walked with him, served him, and stayed close.

Proximity isn't only physical; it's spiritual, emotional, and positional. Many are around greatness but are not aligned to receive. You must position your heart near the one God has anointed for your destiny.

"And Elijah said unto Elisha, Tarry here, I pray thee; for the LORD hath sent me to Bethel. And Elisha said unto him, As the LORD liveth, and as thy soul liveth, I will not leave thee. So they went down to Bethel."
2 Kings 2:2

Distance in the spirit equals disconnection. Impartation flows through closeness.

3. THE LAW OF SERVICE

You receive by serving, not spectating. Elisha poured water on the hands of Elijah. Joshua served Moses. Timothy assisted Paul. The posture of a true son is one of service. You don't serve to be seen; you serve because the grace you honor is the grace that flows.

"And if ye have not been faithful in that which is another man's, who shall give you that which is your own?"
Luke 16:12

You inherit what you honor and steward.

4. THE LAW OF OBEDIENCE

Impartation demands action, not just desire. When Elijah told Elisha, "If you see me when I am taken, it will be yours," it

EIGHT // THE LAWS OF IMPARTATION

wasn't a passive statement. It was a test of obedience, consistency, and spiritual sensitivity. Obedience unlocks access. Consider Mary, the mother of our Lord, at the wedding feast in Cana.

"His mother saith unto the servants, Whatsoever He saith unto you, do it."
John 2:5

Sometimes the instruction looks small, but it is the gateway to massive impartation.

5. THE LAW OF SACRIFICE

The deeper the grace, the greater the price. There are realms you cannot enter without letting go of something, whether it be comfort, pride, possessions, or even reputation. When Elisha followed Elijah, he burned his plow and oxen. He left everything familiar to pursue something eternal.

"But the king replied to Araunah, 'No, I insist on paying you for it. I will not sacrifice to the LORD my God burnt offerings that cost me nothing." So David bought the threshing floor and the oxen and paid fifty shekels of silver for them."
2 Samuel 24:24 NIV

True impartation requires seed, surrender, and sacrifice.

6. THE LAW OF HUNGER

Only the hungry are filled. Desire draws virtue. If you don't burn for more, you won't attract more. Many sit under powerful vessels but receive nothing because they are passively present. Hunger makes you pursue, press in, and pull virtue.

"Blessed are they which do hunger and thirst after righteousness: for they shall be filled."
Matthew 5:6

Hunger is the spiritual magnet that draws impartation.

7. THE LAW OF CONTINUITY

Impartation is sustained through fellowship, instruction, and continuity. Some receive grace but lose it because they disconnect too early. Elijah said, *"If you see me when I'm taken…"* meaning, *stay until the end.* Joshua did not stop serving until Moses was taken. Impartation is not a moment; impartation is a process.

"And let us not be weary in well doing: for in due season we shall reap, if we faint not."
Galatians 6:9

Staying planted preserves the oil.

8. THE LAW OF SPIRITUAL FATHERHOOD

Mantles flow through generational alignment. You receive more than information from a spiritual father; you receive DNA. Paul told Timothy to "stir up the gift" that came through his laying on of hands. Gifts are passed, not just prayed into existence.

EIGHT // THE LAWS OF IMPARTATION

"For though ye have ten thousand instructors in Christ, yet have ye not many fathers: for in Christ Jesus I have begotten you through the gospel."
1 Corinthians 4:15

Fathers give you something mentors cannot: inheritance.

Nine
MYSTERIES AND SECRETS

NINE // MYSTERIES AND SECRETS

"Humble yourselves therefore under the mighty hand of God, that He may exalt you in due time."
1 Peter 5:6

Humility is a spiritual law. It is not just a nice trait; rather, it is a divine requirement for those who seek to be used by God. Without it, elevation in the spirit is not possible. Notice that Peter does not say "God will humble you," but "humble yourselves." It is a conscious act of surrender. To humble yourself under God's mighty hand is to acknowledge His supremacy, His wisdom, and His timing. It is to submit your will, your desires, and even your understanding under His authority, trusting that in His perfect time, He will lift you.

Humility tells God, "I recognize You as the source. I do not promote myself. I do not rely on my own strength. I do not assume I have arrived." This posture attracts divine grace.

"But He giveth more grace. Wherefore He saith, God resisteth the proud, but giveth grace unto the humble."
James 4:6

Grace flows to the humble because the humble are positioned to receive. They know they need God. They live in dependence, not arrogance. Not only that, but true humility also shows in how we relate to people, especially those God has placed over us. Many claim they are submitted to God but carry rebellion in their hearts toward human authority. That is deception. God often tests your humility toward Him by how you treat those He has set above you.

Let's look again at 1 Samuel chapter 3:

"And the child Samuel ministered unto the LORD before Eli. And the word of the LORD was precious in those days; there was

no open vision."
1 Samuel 3:1

Samuel, though called from the womb, did not start his prophetic journey by standing on a mountain and declaring, "Thus saith the Lord." He served and ministered unto the Lord, but before Eli; meaning, under Eli's oversight. Though Eli's own spiritual sight was dimming, God still honored the structure He had set. He allowed Samuel to grow and be trained in that environment. Why? Because humility precedes hearing.

The verse goes on to say, *"the word of the LORD was precious in those days; there was no open vision."* God was not speaking publicly, but He chose to speak privately to a child who had been humbling himself in service. The absence of open vision didn't stop the flow of personal revelation, because Samuel's posture attracted divine attention.

Even when Samuel first heard God's voice, he thought it was Eli. He ran to his authority. That says something powerful about Samuel's posture. He had no assumption that God would bypass order to speak to him. It took Eli's instruction for Samuel to recognize the voice of God. Imagine that! A faulty priest still being used by God to guide a future prophet.

Many today want open visions without the discipline of submission. They want spiritual authority without serving under it. They want to be exalted without ever kneeling. In the Kingdom of God, elevation comes through lowering. Glory comes through humility.

The Scriptures say of the Lord Jesus:

"And being found in fashion as a man, He humbled himself, and became obedient unto death, even the death of the cross. Wherefore God also hath highly exalted Him, and given Him a

NINE // MYSTERIES AND SECRETS

name which is above every name."
Philippians 2:8-9

If our Master had to humble Himself before being exalted, how much more must we?

"Therefore Eli said unto Samuel, Go, lie down: and it shall be, if He call thee, that thou shalt say, Speak, Lord; for Thy servant heareth. So Samuel went and lay down in his place."
1 Samuel 3:9

This verse holds a mystery that many overlook. Though Samuel was the one whom God had chosen to speak to, it was Eli who held the code. Eli, even in his spiritual decline, still carried the understanding of divine protocol. He had walked with God for years. He knew the voice Samuel was hearing, even though it was no longer coming to him. And instead of becoming jealous or insecure, Eli gave Samuel the key: *"Say, Speak, Lord; for thy servant heareth."*

Now consider this: had Samuel been proud, arrogant, or rebellious toward Eli, the high priest would have been under no obligation to unlock that mystery for him. The voice of God would have continued to call, but Samuel would have had no language to respond. This is because the prophetic, though supernatural in nature, is stewarded and passed on through honor and humility, not entitlement.

God had rejected Eli's house, yes, but He had not stripped Eli of his wisdom. God had passed judgment, but He did not revoke spiritual protocol. The transfer did not happen by force or assumption; it came by grace. Grace opened the door, and humility walked through it.

This is where many in this generation falter. They mistake gifting for authority, and assume that the anointing can substitute spiritual experience and bypass divine structure. It is paramount that we understand this about our God: He is not a God of shortcuts.

> *"Wisdom is the principal thing; therefore get wisdom: and with all thy getting get understanding."*
> Proverbs 4:7

The prophetic ministry is not merely about receiving words or having visions; it is about understanding the ways of God, and that understanding is often imparted, not invented. There are divine mysteries that can only be passed on through spiritual fathers, mentors, and covering.

Sadly, if many of today's prophetic voices had an Eli in their life, they would resist him. They would say, "You are not anointed like me," or, "God speaks to me, not to you." They would mistake correction for competition and treat counsel as control. If Eli said to them, "Go lie down," they would think he was trying to delay their destiny, when in truth, he was positioning them for divine encounter.

Samuel honored Eli. Even after hearing the voice of God, he still ran to Eli. That humility positioned him for the next instruction. You cannot hear clearly from Heaven if your ears are closed on Earth. God honors the humble, but He resists the proud. Even the prophetically gifted proud.

Let this be a warning and a call: do not despise the vessels God used to raise you, even if they no longer burn with the same fire. There are mantles that only fall when honor is present. There are revelations that only flow through submission. And there are seasons that only unlock when you lie down where Eli told you.

Stay humble. Stay teachable. Because in the prophetic, access is not just granted by gift; it is passed down through grace.

NINE // MYSTERIES AND SECRETS

THE SPIRITUAL SUBMISSION OF MOSES TO JETHRO

13 And it came to pass on the morrow, that Moses sat to judge the people: and the people stood by Moses from the morning unto the evening.
14 And when Moses' father in law saw all that he did to the people, he said, What is this thing that thou doest to the people? why sittest thou thyself alone, and all the people stand by thee from morning unto even?
15 And Moses said unto his father in law, Because the people come unto me to enquire of God:
16 When they have a matter, they come unto me; and I judge between one and another, and I do make them know the statutes of God, and his laws.
17 And Moses' father in law said unto him, The thing that thou doest is not good.
18 Thou wilt surely wear away, both thou, and this people that is with thee: for this thing is too heavy for thee; thou art not able to perform it thyself alone.
19 Hearken now unto my voice, I will give thee counsel, and God shall be with thee: Be thou for the people to God-ward, that thou mayest bring the causes unto God:
20 And thou shalt teach them ordinances and laws, and shalt shew them the way wherein they must walk, and the work that they must do.
21 Moreover thou shalt provide out of all the people able men, such as fear God, men of truth, hating covetousness; and place such over them, to be rulers of thousands, and rulers of hundreds, rulers of fifties, and rulers of tens:
22 And let them judge the people at all seasons: and it shall be, that every great matter they shall bring unto thee, but every small matter they shall judge: so shall it be easier for thyself, and they

shall bear the burden with thee.
23 If thou shalt do this thing, and God command thee so, then thou shalt be able to endure, and all this people shall also go to their place in peace.
24 So Moses hearkened to the voice of his father in law, and did all that he had said.
Exodus 18:13-24

Moses, the prophet of prophets; the man who spoke with God face to face, who parted seas, called down plagues, and climbed Mount Sinai to commune with the Almighty in fire and thunder. In all the history of prophetic encounters, none stood like Moses except for Jesus Christ, the very God whom Moses met on the mountain, later manifested in flesh.

Yet, with all the power, authority, and grace Moses carried, he was not without spiritual covering. Moses, the great deliverer of Israel, remained submitted to his spiritual father, Jethro, the priest of Midian. It was through this submission and faithful service that Moses became a son in the house of Reuel.

This is where many miss a foundational principle of the prophetic: submission precedes elevation, and ranking in the Spirit is not measured by visible power, but by divine order and protocol.

In Exodus 18:13-24, we witness something profound. Moses is judging the people from morning till evening. He is operating in his gift, leading, teaching, discerning, and guiding the nation of Israel. When Jethro sees this, however, he does not flatter Moses. He corrects him.

"The thing that thou doest is not good…thou wilt surely wear away." This moment is crucial. Jethro sees what Moses cannot. Despite all Moses' intimacy with God, there were things God did not teach him directly. Why? Because some instructions are not given from Heaven; they are passed through spiritual fathers. These are mysteries of longevity,

NINE // MYSTERIES AND SECRETS

principles of leadership, and wisdoms born from walking with God over time.

Jethro says, *"Hearken now unto my voice, I will give thee counsel, and God shall be with thee."* Jethro was not competing with Moses. He wasn't trying to be relevant. He was speaking from a place of authority, age, and spiritual ranking. And Moses, though operating on a higher level of supernatural manifestation, did not resist. He did not argue. He did not dismiss the instruction as outdated or irrelevant. He submitted.

> *"So Moses hearkened to the voice of his father in law, and did all that he had said."*

Let that sink in: Moses hearkened. He didn't simply listen; he obeyed. There was no pride, no rebuttal. No, "But God didn't tell me that." Moses honored the voice of the one who had walked with God before he ever met the burning bush.

This is where our generation struggles. We see young prophets who carry the anointing but lack the humility to be corrected. Many assume that if their fathers don't move in power, they can't speak into their lives. Yet the ranking of the Spirit is not measured by miracles, it is measured by history with God, faithfulness, and spiritual protocol. Power does not replace order. Revelation does not cancel accountability. A son who is truly spiritual knows how to discern the voice of wisdom in his father, even when his father doesn't operate on the same platform of manifestation.

If Moses, God's personal prophet, could be corrected by Jethro, what excuse do we have? And let us not forget: the counsel Jethro gave Moses did not only save Moses, but it preserved the nation.

> *"If thou shalt do this thing, and God command thee so, then thou shalt be able to endure, and all this people shall also go to their place in peace."*

Wisdom flowing through submission brings peace to those under your leadership.

HUMILITY: THE PATHWAY TO PROPHETIC DEPTH

Many think humility is weakness, but humility is actually spiritual intelligence. It is the attitude of those destined to become custodians of God's secrets, those whom Heaven can trust with mighty prophetic manifestations. Before God entrusts revelation, He examines posture. The proud may have flashes of insight, but the humble are given access to deep chambers in the Spirit.

The prophetic is not sustained by gift alone. It is preserved and multiplied through character, and the chief among prophetic character traits is humility. As a born prophet, my greatest advantage has never been the accuracy of my visions or the fire of my declarations. Rather, it has always been my willingness to submit to every authority God placed in my life. That posture of humility has been my open door, granting me the privilege of learning where others assume they already know. This has allowed me to grow where others remain stagnant in their gifting, and as a result made me to be more effective. Not just anointed, but effective in my office as a prophet.

There are things God will never reveal to the arrogant. Not because He is withholding them, but because their hearts cannot carry the weight of His secrets without using them to exalt themselves.

> *"The secret of the Lord is with them that fear Him; and He will shew them His covenant."*
> Psalm 25:14

NINE // MYSTERIES AND SECRETS

Reverence births access. Submission maintains it. Pride forfeits it. Many want the glory of the prophetic, but not the process. They seek the throne without learning how to kneel. In the Kingdom of God, those who kneel longest are raised highest. I have learned that prophetic rank is not in your voice but in your spirit, and spirits are weighed in the presence of God, not in public platforms.

The mantle may be divine, but the discipline to carry it is learned through submission to God, to mentors, to correction, and to order. I have never outgrown the need for authority in my life. Even now, I remain a student, because the moment I stop submitting is the moment I stop ascending. Humility is the key. Submission is the gate. Honor is the ladder. Through these, God will reveal Himself, not just *through* you, but *to* you.

THE REWARDS OF SUBMISSION: A PERSONAL TESTIMONY

My journey in the prophetic has been shaped not by ambition but by submission. Before I was known by multitudes, I was trained in the shadows. Before I stood on platforms, I served at the feet of fathers.

One of those fathers was Reverend Simon Ngizulu, a mighty vessel of God through whom I learned the deep mysteries of deliverance and healing. Though he was my uncle by blood, in the Spirit, he became my father, teacher, and trainer. He gave me no special treatment. There was no shortcut or entitlement. I had to earn my place through service, obedience, and faithfulness.

He would often say to me, *"My son, I am hard on you because of where God is taking you."* I didn't fully understand it then, but now I see the wisdom of his words. Every task he gave me, no matter how small, was a test, a training ground, and a prophetic mirror of what God would one day entrust to me. He taught me that effectiveness in small things was a reflection of how God would use me in greater things. He taught me discipline, order, excellence, and spiritual sensitivity. He corrected me when I fell short and challenged me to rise higher when I became comfortable. He saw the seed of greatness, but he would not allow it to grow without rooting it in humility.

As he watched my consistency, my hunger, and my quiet growth, he began to pour into me and to teach me how to do what he did. He taught me how to cast out devils, how to bring healing to the broken, how to discern spirits, and how to walk with God in power and purity. Because of that foundation, and because I chose to submit in my early teens rather than chase recognition, I now carry a grace that brings healing and deliverance to millions around the world.

This is the divine pattern. Before Jesus ministered to the world, He submitted to Joseph and Mary. Before Elisha took up Elijah's mantle, he poured water on his hands. Before Samuel became God's mouthpiece, he served under Eli. And before I became a prophet to nations, I was a son in the house of Reverend Ngizulu.

You cannot carry glory if you have not been broken. You cannot lead if you have not served. And you will never walk in the fullness of your call unless you are willing to be taught, be corrected, and be shaped by fathers.

My testimony is proof: submission is not bondage; it is preparation. And honor will take you where talent never could.

NINE // MYSTERIES AND SECRETS

THE SECRET OF MY ELEVATION: SERVING THE PROPHET WITHOUT EXPECTATION

If there is one principle that has carried me into prophetic greatness, it is this: submission without expectation. Not submission for promotion. Not service for status. But submission purely out of love for God and honor for His vessels. That has always been my secret.

In my early twenties, I came across a mighty man of God, a seer, a prophet whose name is known across nations. He is a father to many prophets, a man whose eyes see beyond time, and a true general in the prophetic. At first, I encountered him through his teachings on YouTube, and after a few months of engaging with his ministry, I was blessed to speak with him directly on Twitter, now called X. By divine orchestration, a connection was made. When he extended an invitation for me to meet him at a meeting in Houston, Texas, I knew that something divine was unfolding.

From that moment, I didn't come as an equal; I came as a son, a servant, and a student. I carried his Bible. I arranged his garments with care and honor, even his undergarments. I took note of what he liked to eat, what he preferred, what strengthened him. I stayed awake when he stayed awake. He would sleep for only three hours, and I had to keep pace, because when a general is moving, a true son does not fall behind.

I served him, not for promotion or for attention, but because I saw the move of God and I wanted to be part of it. I didn't ask for money or reward. Yes, the Prophet would bless me at times, but my motive was never compensation. My desire was to be near the fire, to be part of what God was doing through this vessel.

Then came the moment that changed everything. One morning, around 5 a.m., while he was in prayer, he called me. I came rushing to his room. What he spoke that day still echoes in my spirit: *"Of all my sons, God has made you great. Your prophetic utterance will increase; you will not be an echo, but a voice. You were born a prophet, but today I also give you my eyes."*

He laid hands on me and imparted vision. From that day, something shifted. The prophetic in me erupted, and my accuracy sharpened. My hearing intensified, and my utterance became weighty. I stepped into a new rank, not just because I was called, but because I was faithful. He taught me the mysteries of the Kingdom. He trained me not just in seeing but in interpreting, discerning, and navigating the corridors of divine knowledge. Today, when prophetic accuracy is discussed, you cannot speak of it without mentioning Prophet Lovy Elias.

Never forget: this elevation did not come by ambition. It came by submission. Quiet, humble, sacrificial submission. I did not push for greatness. I simply served with love, and God, through the mouth of my father, lifted me.

Afterwards, the Lord led me to serve under another prophet, a man of unmatched prophetic depth and divine revelation. His accuracy is beyond sight, piercing realms. To me, he is not only a prophet, but a spiritual father whose walk with God has carved out supernatural pathways I am privileged to walk upon. Serving under him has added layers to my prophetic journey that can only come from alignment with a seasoned mantle.

Before divine prosperity ever found me, I knew what it meant to struggle. In the early days of my ministry, I was sustained by the mercy of God; but I had not yet tapped into covenant prosperity, where I could not only have enough for myself, but enough for those around me. I knew what it meant to stretch, to trust, and to survive.

There came a moment that tested the very core of my obedience and faith, when I had an opportunity to buy a home for my young family. It was a beautiful door, but the funds I had were not enough. Still, the Lord whispered, *"Put in the offer."* And I did. I was given a few

NINE // MYSTERIES AND SECRETS

days to show proof of funds. The clock was ticking, and the money hadn't come. It was Friday, and my heart trembled. *Had I missed God?* In my fear, I called my father, and told him what the Lord had spoken. He asked me one question, *"Do you believe that I hear from God?"* I answered, *"Yes, I do."* Then he said, *"The Lord says, give me what you have as a sign of trust in Him."* This was the only money I had left for my family. It was all I had. Nevertheless, I obeyed. I cleared my account and gave every cent. Not out of pressure, but out of faith in the word of my father and in the God who speaks through him.

I told my wife, Maggy Elias, what I had done. Her response was full of quiet faith: *"Honey, God will not fail us, even though I don't know how He will come through."* That night, the Lord gave me a vision. He said, *"By this afternoon, you will know that I am the Lord your God."*

The next morning, my phone rang. It was a number I didn't recognize. I answered, and the man on the line was overflowing with joy. *"You prayed for me and my family months ago,"* he said. I couldn't remember him, but his words shook me: *"The Lord told me to give you $150,000, and I'm at the bank right now. I'm ready to transfer it to you."*

At first, I thought it was a prank, but by 12 noon, the money hit my account. It was just as God had spoken, not a moment late. Heaven had moved, and the transaction was complete. In that moment, a chain broke, not just in my bank account, but in my bloodline.

From that day, the mystery of divine prosperity was sealed in my life. The days of scraping, hoping, and just surviving were over. The covenant had been activated, not by begging nor by striving, but by obedience and honor.

This is what people miss: *Humility and submission give you access to secrets that cannot be taught in sermons, but must be transferred by experience, through alignment with those who have walked with God.*

You can quote scriptures about abundance. You can fast and pray for breakthrough. But if your heart is not submitted, if your ears are not tuned to the voice of a spiritual father, and if your hands are not open to obey, you will delay what Heaven is trying to deliver. There are mysteries of wealth, principles of multiplication, and keys of Kingdom economics that only fathers who have walked with God can teach, not just in theory, but with manifestation.

Ten
PROPHETIC CONSCIOUSNESS

TEN // PROPHETIC CONSCIOUSNESS

To be conscious means much more than merely existing. Consciousness involves cultivating a state of heightened awareness, being fully present and deeply attentive. When it comes to the prophetic, this heightened awareness is not just beneficial; it is essential. Without finely-tuned spiritual consciousness, you risk missing critical moments when heaven intersects earth, and divine encounters unfold.

Spiritual activity frequently moves swiftly and subtly on this side of the veil. God may speak in a gentle whisper, angels might move quietly within your environment, and even demonic influences can operate unnoticed. Many remain oblivious to these spiritual interactions, failing to discern pivotal moments that could shape their destiny.

This spiritual insensitivity was never part of God's original design for humanity. Mankind lost this profound awareness through ignorance, pride, and broken fellowship. Pride dulls spiritual perception, ignorance obscures understanding, and fractured intimacy with the Holy Spirit distances us from the tangible presence of God.

PROPHETIC CONSCIOUSNESS IN BIBLICAL HISTORY

Throughout biblical history, the prophetic has served as God's bridge to humanity, a sacred channel through which divine secrets, insights, and directives flow. Prophets stood as spiritual gatekeepers, responsible not only for receiving revelation but also for interpreting its deeper meaning to guide individuals and nations alike.

The story of Cain reveals an important spiritual paradox. After murdering Abel, Cain retained a striking level of spiritual consciousness and ability to hear clearly from God:

"And the Lord said unto Cain, Where is Abel thy brother? And he said, I know not: Am I my brother's keeper?
And He said, What hast thou done? The voice of thy brother's blood crieth unto me from the ground."
Genesis 4:9-10

Cain inherited the ability to hear God from his parents, Adam and Eve, who originally walked in perfect intimacy with God. Yet their disobedience in Eden resulted in the loss of their spiritual sight and clarity, leaving them with a diminished spiritual inheritance, hearing without seeing. Cain, whose name means "another man" rather than "a new man," was born under these inherited spiritual defects. Unlike Adam, who was initially created pure and unblemished, Cain carried the compromised spiritual inheritance of fallen humanity. Still, he was able to hear God even after killing his brother.

We thank God, our Father, for the second Adam, Jesus Christ, who creates us anew, born not of defective lineage but of holiness and purity. Unlike Cain, we are reborn spiritually pure, modeled after Jesus Christ, who knew no sin. This means, we should have an advantage when it comes to hearing God.

The Apostle Paul further illustrates the concept that spiritual gifts and capacities can be biologically inherited:

"When I call to remembrance the unfeigned faith that is in thee, which dwelt first in thy grandmother Lois, and thy mother Eunice; and I am persuaded that in thee also.
Wherefore I put thee in remembrance that thou stir up the gift of God, which is in thee by the putting on of my hands.
For God hath not given us the spirit of fear; but of power, and of love, and of a sound mind."
2 Timothy 1:5-7

TEN // PROPHETIC CONSCIOUSNESS

This scripture clearly reveals Timothy inherited spiritual faith and gifting through his bloodline, emphasizing the profound impact of biological inheritance on spiritual gifting.

SAMUEL: A CONTRAST IN PROPHETIC RESPONSE

Contrast Cain sharply with the young prophet Samuel, whose story begins during a spiritually dry era in Israel.

> *"And the child Samuel ministered unto the Lord before Eli. And the word of the Lord was precious in those days; there was no open vision."*
> 1 Samuel 3:1

This highlights a time of spiritual scarcity, making Samuel's eventual prophetic experiences uniquely significant. Samuel, unlike Cain, was graced not only with hearing but also with clear visionary encounters.

Samuel inherited a more complete prophetic gifting from Eli, his spiritual father. Although Eli himself had grown spiritually dim due to age and familial negligence, he retained enough discernment to guide Samuel into prophetic maturity, demonstrating that spiritual gifts can be passed through spiritual mentorship, even when imperfect.

Initially unaware of the personal voice of God, Samuel mistook divine speech for Eli's voice:

> *"And the LORD called Samuel again the third time. And he arose and went to Eli, and said, Here am I; for thou didst call me. And Eli perceived that the LORD had called the child.*

> *Therefore Eli said unto Samuel, Go, lie down: and it shall be, if He call thee, that thou shalt say, Speak, LORD; for Thy servant heareth. So Samuel went and lay down in his place.*
> *And the LORD came, and stood, and called as at other times, Samuel, Samuel. Then Samuel answered, Speak; for Thy servant heareth."*
> 1 Samuel 3:8-10

Samuel's humility and teachability positioned him for deeper prophetic revelation. It took spiritual discernment on Eli's part to perceive that it was the Lord calling the boy. With that recognition came instruction: *"Speak, Lord, for your servant hears."*

What follows is profound: *"And the Lord came, and stood, and called..."* God did not merely speak; He came, He stood, and He called. This wasn't just an audible moment; it was a visitation. Samuel, now positioned by instruction and prepared by humility, responded correctly: "Speak; for Thy servant heareth."

Through these accounts, we observe two very distinct prophetic experiences:

- Cain heard and deflected; Samuel heard and responded.
- Cain spoke with arrogance; Samuel answered with humility.
- Cain's awareness was corrupted by guilt; Samuel's was nurtured through guidance.

This passage teaches us that:

- Spiritual activity is not always accompanied by understanding.
- Sensitivity must be trained through guidance and instruction.

TEN // PROPHETIC CONSCIOUSNESS

- Divine calling often comes in the midst of service and obedience.
- God waits for a prepared response before revealing deeper things.

This contrast highlights several crucial truths, a fundamental one being: spiritual inheritance profoundly affects prophetic capacity. Prophetic awareness must be intentionally cultivated, and true intimacy with God requires recognition and correct response. Thus, we learn:

- Spiritual nearness does not guarantee spiritual knowing.
- Prophetic awareness must be cultivated through instruction.
- Intimacy with God begins with recognition, then response.
- The prophetic life is not about hearing alone; it is about knowing the One who speaks.

LESSONS FROM SAUL AND DAVID

The stories of Saul and David emphasize how critical our responses to God's voice are. Saul responded to confrontation with excuses, losing his kingdom:

> *"And Saul said unto Samuel, Yea, I have obeyed the voice of the LORD, and have gone the way which the LORD sent me, and have brought Agag the king of Amalek, and have utterly destroyed the Amalekites.*
> *But the people took of the spoil, sheep and oxen, the chief of the things which should have been utterly destroyed, to sacrifice unto the LORD thy God in Gilgal.*

> *And Samuel said, Hath the LORD as great delight in burnt offerings and sacrifices, as in obeying the voice of the LORD? Behold, to obey is better than sacrifice, and to hearken than the fat of rams."*
> 1 Samuel 15:20-22

David, by contrast, responded with genuine repentance, securing God's continued favor:

> *"And David said unto Nathan, I have sinned against the Lord. And Nathan said unto David, The Lord also hath put away thy sin; thou shalt not die."*
> 2 Samuel 12:13

Hearing God initiates our prophetic journey, but our response determines its direction and fulfillment.

A CALL TO INTIMACY AND ALIGNMENT

Samuel's journey from servant to Seer began with one humble phrase: "Speak, Lord, for thy servant heareth." This humility contrasts Cain's defensive response, illustrating that prophetic consciousness alone is inadequate without alignment to God's heart.

Thus, true prophetic consciousness demands humility, intentional cultivation, and responsive obedience. Through Christ, the second Adam, we can inherit purity, clarity, and a prophetic life free from defect, confidently embracing our divine calling.

Eleven
MASTERING THE FLOW OF THE SPIRIT

ELEVEN // MASTERING THE FLOW OF THE SPIRIT

NAVIGATING DIVINE CURRENTS AND PROPHETIC STREAMS

Mastering the prophetic flow is essential for consistently ministering God's will. Many misunderstand that fully walking in the prophetic isn't only about God speaking to you; it is equally rooted in your dialogue and inquiry with God on behalf of those around you.

When we achieve this mastery, we enter what I like to call "God mode," the extraordinary capacity to transition seamlessly from natural realities into the divine presence of God Almighty. You can physically be among people yet spiritually translated into heavenly realms, fully aware of the natural world. In this profound dimension, we display the glory of God not merely through words but by stepping into realms of power and the Spirit, as the Apostle Paul mentions in

> *"And my speech and my preaching was not with enticing words of man's wisdom, but in demonstration of the Spirit and of power: That your faith should not stand in the wisdom of men, but in the power of God."*
> 1 Corinthians 2:4-5

Within this dimension, you gain access to miracles and supernatural solutions, not solely through prayer, but through authoritative prophetic decrees and instructions which God Himself backs and honors according to your word. A beautiful example of "God mode" is found in the account of Peter and John going to the temple:

> *"Then Peter said, Silver and gold have I none; but such as I have give I thee: In the name of Jesus Christ of Nazareth rise up and walk. And he took him by the right hand, and lifted him up: and*

immediately his feet and ankle bones received strength. And he leaping up stood, and walked, and entered with them into the temple, walking, and leaping, and praising God."
Acts 3:6-8

What Peter achieved was due to his arrival at the place of prophetic mastery, or what we call "God mode." With a single word, God manifests Himself in any situation. Ultimately, the fullness of the prophetic is the ability to express the Lord Jesus Christ in His entirety. As one of my favorite prophets famously declared, there is no sickness that the Lord Jesus cannot cure, no disease He cannot heal, and no situation He cannot resolve. This is the dimension we must aspire to when we operate in the prophetic.

"God mode" is often misunderstood by many believers because the ways those empowered by God operate can appear unusual or even be mistaken as witchcraft, though it absolutely is not. The Apostle Paul clarifies this in Scripture.

"And there are differences of administrations, but the same Lord. And there are diversities of operations, but it is the same God which worketh all in all."
1 Corinthians 12:5-6

Prophetic examples throughout scripture clearly illustrate this principle. Elisha instructed Naaman to dip himself seven times in the river, resulting in complete restoration.

"So Naaman came with his horses and with his chariot, and stood at the door of the house of Elisha.
And Elisha sent a messenger unto him, saying, Go and wash in Jordan seven times, and thy flesh shall come again to thee, and

ELEVEN // MASTERING THE FLOW OF THE SPIRIT

thou shalt be clean."
2 Kings 5:9-10

At another time, Elisha cast salt into the waters with a prophetic decree, and they were healed.

> *"And the men of the city said unto Elisha, Behold, I pray thee, the situation of this city is pleasant, as my lord seeth: but the water is naught, and the ground barren.*
> *And he said, Bring me a new cruse, and put salt therein. And they brought it to him.*
> *And he went forth unto the spring of the waters, and cast the salt in there, and said, Thus saith the LORD, I have healed these waters; there shall not be from thence any more death or barren land.*
> *So the waters were healed unto this day, according to the saying of Elisha which he spake."*
> 2 Kings 2:19-22

Moses threw wood into bitter waters, rendering them drinkable

> *"And the people murmured against Moses, saying, What shall we drink?*
> *And he cried unto the LORD; and the LORD shewed him a tree, which when he had cast into the waters, the waters were made sweet: there He made for them a statute and an ordinance, and there He proved them."*
> Exodus 15:24-25

These actions were not mere symbolic acts but authoritative prophetic decrees activating miracles and fulfilling God's word.

One night during prayer, I shared with the Lord my concern

about people unable to travel to receive prayer, particularly for barrenness. The Lord instructed me to use apples, telling those who desired children that the number of seeds represented how many children they could have if they believed. Acting on this instruction, many in our church experienced miraculous pregnancies. Even online viewers purchased apples, prayed alongside, and witnessed divine miracles.

Mastering the flow of the Spirit of Prophecy enables us to be solution-oriented rather than problem-focused. Our motivation for prayer must stem from God's prompting and not be driven by the noise around us.

SPIRITUAL FLOW OF POWER

Mastery is crucial for understanding how the power of God flows through a person. This knowledge comes exclusively through experience and divine revelation, often taking seasoned prophets extensive time and dedication to fully manifest. It demands significant spiritual discipline to reach such a place of divine manifestation.

Imagine a small creek flowing downhill, forming pools along its path. Even though gravity naturally aids its flow, trash thrown into the creek will obstruct the current, frustrating the natural movement of water. Increasing the volume of water won't remove the obstruction; instead, it creates swampy areas where harmful insects and creatures make their homes.

The trash symbolizes the pollution of the members of our bodies, which should be fully consecrated to God. This pollution isn't limited to sin alone; it also includes defilement through using our members for things not intended for them. The insects represent demonic entities actively working to hinder and destroy the gifts of God within us, leading us to feel frustrated and conflicted within our own giftings. The swampy areas illustrate spiritual stagnation, preventing us from excelling or progressing beyond our current spiritual state.

This vividly portrays believers who quote the scripture, "out of their bellies shall flow rivers of living water," yet exhibit no supernatural manifestation. Though we possess the life of the Lord Jesus Christ and His resurrection power within us, many fail to manifest these realities because they do not understand how the Spirit of God flows through them to produce prophetic virtues capable of transforming the world.

The spirit of prophecy flows similarly to the anointing oil poured over Aaron, covering him from head to feet symbolizing that all our members should be fully surrendered for the Lord's divine expressions.

INSTRUMENTS OF THE SPIRIT

Understanding the members of your physical body and their role in the prophetic is absolutely vital. Each part must be intentionally consecrated for the Master's use; otherwise, it becomes impossible for the Holy Spirit to fully express Himself through you. The Holy Spirit not only requires the cooperation of your spirit and soul, He also needs your body.

Why? Because for most people, spiritual realities remain invisible and intangible without physical expression. Your body serves as the vessel, the tangible point of contact, allowing the spiritual dimension to become visible, audible, and experiential to others. In the prophetic, your hands, eyes, ears, mouth, even your posture and movements become divine instruments through which heaven speaks, heals, and transforms.

Mismanagement or neglect of any part of your physical body makes it difficult, perhaps even impossible, to fully express God, despite Him being with you. When you carefully observe the realm of the spirit, certain truths become clear. Consider this: a spirit of stealing cannot effectively possess someone who lacks eyes or hands. Why? Because when this evil spirit injects envy or jealousy into the individual's soul, how can that person act upon the desire to steal without eyes to covet or hands to take? How can he manifest the intent of that spirit?

In the same manner, the Holy Spirit also requires the consecration and sanctification of our physical members. Your eyes, your ears, your mouth, your hands; they all must be purified and set apart because they become His tools. Without a body yielded to Him, the Spirit's divine expression remains locked within, unseen and unheard by those who desperately need His touch.

As believers, we must understand that Satan tirelessly works overtime to silence and render the children of God ineffective. We live in a spiritual war zone, with landmines and fiery darts of deception flying everywhere, strategically designed to conform us to this world and the patterns of those bound by its reality. Yet, the Scriptures declare clearly:

> *"I have given them thy word; and the world hath hated them, because they are not of the world, even as I am not of the world. I pray not that thou shouldest take them out of the world, but that thou shouldest keep them from the evil.*
> *They are not of the world, even as I am not of the world."*
> John 17:14-16

ELEVEN // MASTERING THE FLOW OF THE SPIRIT

Demonic entities exist called principalities; these are fallen spirits assigned to territories, regions, and nations. Apostle Paul explicitly warns us of this reality:

> *"For we wrestle not against flesh and blood, but against principalities, against powers, against the rulers of the darkness of this world, against spiritual wickedness in high places."*
> Ephesians 6:12

These demonic principalities strategically operate to destroy believers by influencing culture, steering fashion, manipulating trends, and distorting societal norms. These evil entities deliberately frustrate and silence God's gifted vessels, those designed to express His heart and power clearly and unmistakably.

We must discern carefully, for the Bible prophetically reveals a dangerous shift in culture and values:

> *"Woe unto them that call evil good, and good evil; that put darkness for light, and light for darkness; that put bitter for sweet, and sweet for bitter!"*
> Isaiah 5:20

Indeed, today we witness openly celebrated abominations; things unimaginable only twenty years ago have become common and accessible. Tragically, many believers unknowingly allow these forces to block, defile, or even destroy the prophetic instruments God placed within them, becoming spiritually blind, deaf, and mute without realizing the damage. We must urgently awaken, reclaim our prophetic purity and authority, and fully consecrate our eyes, ears, mouths, and hands. These members of our bodies are sacred instruments God intends to powerfully use to manifest His Kingdom and glory in the earth.

BODILY PORTALS

Your body is divided into three distinct yet interconnected parts: the physical body, the soul body, and the spirit body. Each possesses its own set of members that intricately link together. Consider a simple yet profound example: your spirit has eyes, your soul also has eyes (though we typically identify these as the eyes of the heart), and your physical body possesses eyes. We observe with our natural eyes but perceive and understand through our heart. When God speaks to us within our spirit, we observe through our spiritual eyes and comprehend deeply within our heart.

Understanding the mechanics of our being is crucial for our bodies to be effectively used by God. Just as Seraphim described in Scripture have eyes covering their bodies (Isaiah 6:2-3), those born of the Spirit also possess multiple avenues of spiritual perception. The book of Revelation vividly depicts the Lord Jesus as a Lamb with seven eyes:

> *"And I beheld, and, lo, in the midst of the throne and of the four beasts, and in the midst of the elders, stood a Lamb as it had been slain, having seven horns and seven eyes, which are the seven Spirits of God sent forth into all the earth."*
> Revelation 5:6

Since we are called to be conformed to His image, we must diligently strive to embody all He intends for us. Only then can we truly become His instruments, operating without hindrance and free from the enemy's infiltration.

Our bodies serve as portals that both receive and release God's spirit and power. An excellent illustration is found in women, who are uniquely designed as portals through which human spirits enter the physical world. Fathers contribute the seed, but mothers are the divine portals allowing human spirits to enter earth. The Lord Jesus required Mary, His mother, to access earth as a human being. His miraculous conception, devoid of human paternal DNA, underscores the portal nature of a woman's body. This profound truth highlights why there is such significant distortion concerning gender and identity today. These distortions, crafted by the enemy, aim to obstruct and disable bodily portals from fulfilling their divine purpose.

There is a profound reason why we must fully grasp that we are divine spirits born of God Himself living in a physical body. Embracing this truth enables us to see our physical bodies as channels of God's virtues. Without this understanding, it becomes impossible to truly walk in the prophetic. Even the seemingly insignificant parts of our bodies play critical roles in spiritual operations. An excellent example is found in Mark chapter 1:

> *"And Jesus, moved with compassion, put forth his hand, and touched him, and saith unto him, I will; be thou clean."*
> Mark 1:41

The word "compassion" here is *splagchnizomai*, a Greek term derived from *splagchna*, referring to internal organs, specifically the bowels or gut. This explains the physical sensations we experience, like butterflies in the stomach when in love, or fear and anxiety causing gastrointestinal distress. Our internal organs can thus express the Spirit of God, our human spirit, or even reflect the state of our soul. For the Lord Jesus, this gut reaction led Him to compassion because it was the Father's will being communicated directly to Him. This underscores why spiritual disciplines such as fasting and abstaining from unclean things and pollution are profoundly important.

DIVINE TOOLS

Just as the Church is described as the body of Christ, so too are the individual members of your body essential, each playing a unique and vital role in ministering God's voice through you. In the early stages of one's prophetic journey, many believers find themselves experiencing firsthand the conditions or emotions of others as they intercede in prayer.

Consider this familiar scenario: as you pray for someone, you might suddenly experience a physical symptom, such as a headache. If you are spiritually attentive and alert, you quickly realize that God is highlighting to you the exact issue afflicting the person you are interceding for. Once you've discerned the message clearly, the symptom promptly disappears. When you inquire, "Have you been experiencing headaches?" the person often responds with amazement, confirming your prophetic insight. Whether the issue is frequent or occasional, this experience confirms that God is indeed speaking to you. This sensitivity highlights the necessity of remaining spiritually alert, fully conscious, and deeply present. Your body, thus, becomes an instrument of divine tools in the hands of the Holy Spirit, allowing you to accurately discern and minister effectively to others through God's guidance.

The divine tools we possess begin with the head, where the brain resides, representing the soul's mind because consciousness and self-awareness exist here. This area houses one of the most significant portals within humanity. For the first two years of a child's life, their crown remains open as their skull gradually closes. During this period, the child's soul and mind receive divine downloads, and most children naturally perceive angels, experiencing spiritual realities as commonplace because their minds remain pure and unpolluted by sin consciousness.

Whenever we pray for others to receive God's blessing,

scripture commands us to lay hands upon them. This practice, often overlooked by believers, is significant because the crown of the head acts as a portal to receive divine impartations. Joshua, for instance, received impartation from Moses through the laying on of hands:

> *"And Joshua the son of Nun was full of the spirit of wisdom; for Moses had laid his hands upon him: and the children of Israel hearkened unto him, and did as the LORD commanded Moses."*
> Deuteronomy 34:9

Laying hands on one's head transfers grace and facilitates receiving information from heaven. Satan, aware of this spiritual dynamic, aggressively seeks to pollute human minds, especially targeting prophets and prophetic individuals to disrupt the divine flow.

The mind serves as the control center for everything entering a person, whether spiritual or natural. A disoriented mind becomes a significant hindrance to the Spirit of God. Scripture clearly states,

> *"The carnal mind is enmity against God: for it is not subject to the law of God, neither indeed can be."*
> Romans 8:7

Therefore, anything prompting us to behave carnally is toxic to our prophetic capacity. Distractions such as Instagram, TikTok, YouTube, and other entertainment platforms saturate our modern world, designed to draw us away from God's presence. While these platforms can indeed serve as tools to advance God's kingdom, we must ensure they do not become our masters. The enemy designs these distractions specifically to diminish our spiritual awareness and obstruct our walk with God.

The remedy for protecting the mind lies in consistent meditation on God's purposes and being fully present and committed with every member of our bodies, recognizing that the mind controls all our bodily functions and spiritual receptivity.

Another vital way we protect the mind is by guarding the spiritual and physical portal known as the ears. This gateway plays a dual role; what enters through the ears has the power to either build faith or corrupt spiritual discernment. Our spiritual ears are designed to hear divine instruction, but they can grow dull when we spend little or no time in God's presence. In the book of Revelation, the Lord repeatedly declares, "He that hath an ear, let him hear what the Spirit saith unto the churches" (Revelation 2:7), revealing that not everyone has ears tuned to perceive the Spirit's voice.

Psalm 107:20 tells us, *"He sent his word, and healed them, and delivered them from their destructions."* We also see in Matthew 8 how Jesus simply spoke a word, and the centurion's servant was healed.

> *"The centurion answered and said, Lord, I am not worthy that thou shouldest come under my roof: but speak the word only, and my servant shall be healed.*
> *For I am a man under authority, having soldiers under me: and I say to this man, Go, and he goeth; and to another, Come, and he cometh; and to my servant, Do this, and he doeth it.*
> *When Jesus heard it, He marvelled, and said to them that followed, Verily I say unto you, I have not found so great faith, no, not in Israel."*
> Matthew 8:8-10

Jesus marveled at the centurion's faith, saying He had not seen such faith in all of Israel. These miracles occurred because those who received them had functioning spiritual faculties; they heard His word with spiritual ears, even at a distance. But what happens when a person lacks this spiritual capacity? They are left to rely solely on their physical ears.

ELEVEN // MASTERING THE FLOW OF THE SPIRIT

When John the Baptist was ministering at the Jordan River, he was startled to see certain groups of people coming for baptism. According to him, the message was not meant for them. He exclaimed, *"O generation of vipers, who hath warned you to flee from the wrath to come?"* (Matthew 3:7). Though he was preaching repentance, he was shocked by their response because only those with spiritual ears can truly hear God's voice through a prophetic vessel.

Our ears, then, are not neutral; they shape our faith or breed confusion based on what we permit to enter. Listening to uplifting, faith-filled words sharpens spiritual sensitivity, while entertaining gossip, slander, or worldly distractions dulls the mind and poisons the soul. Don't become a dumping ground for the noise and pollution of others. Many cannot hear God because their ears are already filled with biased opinions or preconceptions about the very people they are called to intercede for. God will not speak where there is no room for His voice.

Tragically, some have lost prophetic clarity because they have chased after trending news and popular voices rather than remaining anchored in the Spirit. They crave prophetic relevance but trade it for spiritual emptiness. A prophetic person must reserve their ears for the voice of the Lord, filtering everything through the lens of edification and truth. Protecting your ears is protecting your mind and it is far better to guard your mind at the gate than to try and purge defilement from your subconscious later.

Our eyes also play a significant role in protecting the mind, as they provide the mind with the capacity to form clear and vivid images. Describing the vastness and beauty of the ocean to someone who has never seen it can be challenging; although words can form images, it is never with the same depth and clarity that sight provides. Many have defiled and corrupted minds because of what they have consistently looked upon.

Consider the time the Lord Jesus walked on water when no boat was available.

> *"And in the fourth watch of the night Jesus went unto them, walking on the sea.*
> *And when the disciples saw Him walking on the sea, they were troubled, saying, It is a spirit; and they cried out for fear.*
> *But straightway Jesus spake unto them, saying, Be of good cheer; it is I; be not afraid.*
> *And Peter answered Him and said, Lord, if it be Thou, bid me come unto Thee on the water. And He said, Come. And when Peter was come down out of the ship, he walked on the water, to go to Jesus."*
> Matthew 14:25-29

In His mind, it was impossible to drown; to Him, the water and dry ground were essentially the same. Despite their physical differences in density and molecular structure, to Jesus, there was no meaningful distinction. Conversely, many people are trapped in fear and unable to see a path forward because they have observed others fail. Their doubts and unbelief block their ability to receive breakthroughs or prophetically impart them to others.

Exposure to harmful images such as pornography, horror films, or frequent scenes of death corrupts and damages the mind, obstructing the body's ability to clearly perceive and communicate what God is revealing. Protecting our eyes, therefore, is crucial to safeguarding our minds and preserving our spiritual sensitivity.

Likewise, if we allow negative things to dominate our minds, even when God speaks, our distorted internal framework will cause us to misinterpret His messages. This leads to confusion, misguidance, and ultimately spiritual death rather than life. Therefore, guarding our minds from negativity is not only wise but crucial for accurately discerning and delivering God's life-giving word to His people.

ELEVEN // MASTERING THE FLOW OF THE SPIRIT

THE VOICE PORTAL

One of the most powerful divine tools at our disposal is the voice. It serves not merely as a physical instrument for communication but also as a profound spiritual portal through which heaven's authority and prophetic power are released. The voice, when yielded to God, becomes a channel for His divine decrees, shifting atmospheres, commanding breakthroughs, and transforming lives.

Most do not understand that the voice is the result of a far more intricate spiritual machinery. Consequently, many people make declarations without seeing results, attempting even to command healing or cast out devils, yet their voices carry no real authority or power, despite declaring scriptural truths.

The apostles, when still disciples of the Lord Jesus, were initially excited because devils obeyed their commands. However, these same disciples later struggled and failed to deliver another individual from demonic influence, prompting them to ask the Lord why they could not cast out the devil, despite having been given power and authority. The Lord Jesus explained,

> *"And He said unto them, This kind can come forth by nothing, but by prayer and fasting."*
> Mark 9:29

Many believers misunderstand this instruction, thinking fasting itself directly casts out devils. Yet fasting alone does not accomplish deliverance. I've witnessed numerous individuals fasting without achieving spiritual breakthroughs. Thankfully, I discovered the deeper mysteries behind this truth. Recall that when John's disciples questioned Jesus about fasting, He replied,

> *"And Jesus said unto them, Can the children of the bridechamber*

fast, while the bridegroom is with them? as long as they have the bridegroom with them, they cannot fast.
But the days will come, when the bridegroom shall be taken away from them, and then shall they fast in those days."
Mark 2:19-20

Later, after their failure, He specifically instructed His disciples to fast. What, then, is the true reason and mystery behind this command? There was no need for them to fast initially because He was physically present with them. His presence alone provided the spiritual clarity, authority, and power they needed. The principle behind the command to fast, therefore, was to prepare them for the time when He would no longer be physically present. Fasting would become essential to align their spirits and souls deeply with God's will and purposes, sharpening their spiritual senses, and ensuring their voices carried genuine authority and power. In other words, fasting isn't primarily about affecting the external environment, but rather about refining the internal spiritual machinery that empowers our voice as a divine portal. Fasting purifies the voice because of the time spent in prayer and the careful use of words.

THE HEART

The heart is the first place from which the voice is generated; it then travels through the throat, mouth, and finally, the lips. Each of these organs contributes uniquely to the voice. If any part of this pathway is corrupted or defiled, what emerges will contaminate the whole being, turning the voice into poison that harms rather than heals or restores.

ELEVEN // MASTERING THE FLOW OF THE SPIRIT

"A good man out of the good treasure of the heart bringeth forth good things: and an evil man out of the evil treasure bringeth forth evil things."
Matthew 12:35

This scripture describes the condition of the heart, emphasizing that from it, a person brings forth either good or evil things. The primary purpose of fasting is to humble and cleanse the soul, because the voice originates from the heart. The Bible clearly states, *"Before they call, I will answer"* (Isaiah 65:24), highlighting the heart's role in determining the intent behind the spoken word.

Many believers carry a defiled heart despite speaking seemingly good words. Some harbor unforgiveness yet hope their voices will be used prophetically by God. This is a grave self-deception. The prophetic journey demands total surrender to God. Merely uttering the right words from a corrupted heart may impress externally but will inevitably disappoint God and make one a subject of mockery by demonic forces, who easily identify darkness within. Therefore, purifying the heart is the foundational step to genuinely empowering the voice, as the heart sets the true intent behind our words.

THE THROAT

"For there is no faithfulness in their mouth; their inward part is very wickedness; their throat is an open sepulchre; they flatter with their tongue."
Psalm 5:9

No life can proceed from a defiled throat. Often times, when people lie, their hearts condemn them internally, causing discomfort as false words pass through their throats. The throat determines the tone and expression of the voice. If a voice lacks truth, it produces a spiritually dead sound, ineffective in the realm of the Spirit. When some people shout in gatherings, a prophetic ear immediately senses the emptiness of their cries, devoid of spiritual substance.

The Bible instructs, *"Make a joyful noise unto the Lord"* (Psalm 100:1), highlighting that true worship, although seemingly noisy to human ears, resonates joyfully in heaven. When the throat is compromised, sound cannot be produced effectively, just as tired vocal cords struggle to produce voice. Similarly, those lacking discipline in prayer experience spiritual fatigue; though their hearts desire prayer, their spiritual throats lack the strength to vocalize their petitions clearly.

> *"For as he thinketh in his heart, so is he: Eat and drink, saith he to thee; but his heart is not with thee."*
> Proverbs 23:7

> *"For like a hair in the throat, so are they. 'Eat and drink!' they say to you; but they do not mean it."*
> Proverbs 23:7 (NRS)

This verse illustrates vividly how outward words may not reflect true inward intent.

THE MOUTH

The mouth shapes the content and quality of the sound created in the throat, much like the body of a guitar. While the neck of the

ELEVEN // MASTERING THE FLOW OF THE SPIRIT

guitar determines the notes, the body produces the sound. The mouth controls volume, softness, and whether sound emerges at all. A dumb spirit can silence a person, preventing them from releasing their voice. This also occurs in demonic spiritual attacks where individuals cannot physically move or call upon the Lord, despite their intent.

Satan often manipulates life's challenges to induce disbelief in God, silencing believers' mouths from speaking truth. God instructed Moses, *"Open thy mouth wide, and I will fill it"* (Psalm 81:10), emphasizing that the mouth is a key place for the voice's manifestation.

> *"For the Lord giveth wisdom: out of His mouth cometh knowledge and understanding."*
> Proverbs 2:6

This shows that every request for understanding is answered by encountering God's mouth, where wisdom and revelation are imparted. Prophet Daniel heard God's voice but initially lacked understanding because he had not yet encountered the realm of divine wisdom imparted directly from God's mouth.

King Solomon exemplified a purified mouth, consistently producing wisdom without contradiction.

> *"Out of the same mouth proceedeth blessing and cursing. My brethren, these things ought not so to be."*
> James 3:10

This verse cautions that blessings and curses should not originate from the same mouth. Scripture also reminds us, *"Even a fool, when he holdeth his peace, is counted wise"* (Proverbs 17:28). In today's world, where everyone seeks to speak and be heard, true power and wisdom lie in knowing when to open our mouths and when to remain silent.

THE TONGUE

The tongue is like the fingers that strum a guitar; without it, there is no voice given to the deep words that reside in one's heart. It is the pen that powerfully writes our spoken words into reality, and the moment our thoughts take shape through our tongue, we must be ready to reap the consequences of those words.

The Scriptures clearly state in Proverbs:

"A wholesome tongue is a tree of life: but perverseness therein is a breach in the spirit."
Proverbs 15:4

Thus, the tongue serves as a tree, bearing fruits that can either nourish life or breed destruction. The degree to which we consecrate this powerful organ profoundly impacts our lives.

In today's world, many celebrate being vocal and expressive; however, spiritual men and women recognize that careless words pose significant risks, not only to the speaker but also to those who hear them. The enemy may provoke us through others, tempting us to utter words capable of harming our families and sabotaging our future. Yet, we are called to manage ourselves differently.

We must consistently question ourselves before speaking: Should I speak these words? Will my words build up or tear down? Our intentional management of the tongue ultimately determines whether our words become instruments of life and blessing or weapons of harm and destruction.

Because the tongue acts as a portal connecting human life to the spiritual world, it is one of the most critical organs in the realm of spiritual influence. Satan specifically seeks to gain control over it, knowing that if he captures your tongue, he can influence your life and the lives of those around you. Confusion and misunderstanding often

ELEVEN // MASTERING THE FLOW OF THE SPIRIT

arise from poor management of our tongues. Even within the church, the house of God, disorder and chaos can prevail due to inadequate control and stewardship of this vital organ.

LIPS

Lips spiritually represent the emotional state, reflecting the condition of one's soul and spirit. An insightful example of this can be observed when an individual is suffering from depression or anxiety; their lips often become chapped, cracked, or even bleed, symbolizing the internal dryness and turmoil they are experiencing. As one of the most sensitive and expressive parts of our body, the lips vividly portray our emotional condition. Trembling lips can indicate fear, distress, or uncertainty, further underscoring their profound connection to our inner spiritual and mental state.

The Scripture emphasizes this profound symbolism clearly:

"Set a watch, O LORD, before my mouth; keep the door of my lips."
Psalm 141:3

Here, the Bible underscores the critical importance of the words that proceed from our mouths, placing special emphasis on the lips as spiritual gates. Lips guard and shape our words, serving as the final expression of the spirit that gives life to speech. Thus, the lips are not merely physical but serve as portals through which the condition and intentions of the heart and spirit are revealed.

"The lip of truth shall be established for ever: but a lying tongue is

but for a moment."
Proverbs 12:19

This verse reveals that while one might attempt deception through words, even deceiving oneself, the lips invariably expose the true nature and spiritual condition within. Truth, when spoken without love, ultimately fails because genuine love must flow through lips that convey comfort, grace, and reassurance, easing the listener into receiving even the most challenging correction. Delivering messages with a genuine, warm smile effectively disarms resistance, aligning the listener's intention and desire toward openness and acceptance.

Hebrews chapter 13 further deepens our understanding, instructing us:

"By Him therefore let us offer the sacrifice of praise to God continually, that is, the fruit of our lips giving thanks to His name."
Hebrews 13:15

Interestingly, the scripture highlights "the fruit of our lips," rather than mentioning the heart or tongue, reinforcing that the lips directly reflect the spiritual state within us. Proverbs chapter 20 echoes this, declaring:

"There is gold, and a multitude of rubies: but the lips of knowledge are a precious jewel."
Proverbs 20:15

Lips expressing the knowledge of God are more precious than the most sought-after jewels, serving as a profound indicator of the spiritual treasures stored within.

This revelation also sheds light on why Judas' betrayal of Jesus

ELEVEN // MASTERING THE FLOW OF THE SPIRIT

was particularly painful.

BETRAYAL BY A KISS

Contrary to popular belief, sex is not the pinnacle of intimacy, affection, or love. Indeed, sex is sacred, divinely ordained to produce life and deepen joy within the covenant of marriage. However, lust can distort even this sacred act, allowing physical desire to masquerade as genuine affection. While intimacy through sexual acts can be feigned, a genuine kiss cannot be easily counterfeited. Though a kiss may also stem from lustful intentions, its purest expression carries profound spiritual significance, encapsulating sincere love and affection for our children, families, and loved ones.

Kissing symbolizes profound peace, love, and joy within familial relationships between fathers, mothers, children, and siblings. In numerous cultures worldwide, including my own, greetings often include a tender kiss on the cheek. This gesture reflects genuine joy, warmth, and affectionate welcome, establishing bonds of heartfelt unity and sincerity.

During the time of our Lord Jesus Christ, kissing held deep cultural and spiritual significance. It was a customary expression of greeting, affection, honor, and respect toward leaders, rulers, and royalty. Even today, traditional religious circles, such as the Catholic and Orthodox churches, uphold this sacred gesture, often demonstrated through reverent kissing of the rings of spiritual authorities. Kissing further symbolized profound devotion and worship, exemplified powerfully in Luke chapter 7:

> *"And stood at His feet behind Him weeping, and began to wash His feet with tears, and did wipe them with the hairs of her head, and kissed His feet, and anointed them with the ointment."*
> Luke 7:38

The Apostle Paul urged believers to greet one another with a holy kiss, recognizing its significance as a spiritual bond and expression of unity within the body of Christ:

> *"Greet one another with an holy kiss."*
> 2 Corinthians 13:12

Yet, one of the darkest episodes in biblical history involved the desecration of this very act of purity. Judas Iscariot's betrayal of our Lord was marked not by an open accusation or overt aggression but by the subtle, deceptive intimacy of a kiss:

> *"But Jesus said unto him, Judas, betrayest thou the Son of man with a kiss?"*
> Luke 22:48

This betrayal carries profound prophetic significance. Judas transformed an act symbolic of purity and devotion into an instrument of treachery and spiritual violation. The Lord's poignant question exposed not only the betrayal itself but also highlighted the depth of Judas's internal corruption. This action broke a fundamental spiritual principle, provoking immediate spiritual conviction and torment in Judas, leading him to despairingly attempt to return the thirty pieces of silver he received for his betrayal, confessing the enormity of his sin:

> *"Then Judas, which had betrayed Him, when he saw that he was condemned, repented himself, and brought again the thirty pieces of silver to the chief priests and elders,*
> *Saying, I have sinned in that I have betrayed the innocent blood. And they said, What is that to us? see thou to that."*
> Matthew 27:3-4

ELEVEN // MASTERING THE FLOW OF THE SPIRIT

This narrative compels us to introspect deeply. Did Judas understand the extent of the darkness residing within him before the betrayal, or did the act of betrayal itself expose his true spiritual condition? The kiss of Judas prophetically underscores the eternal truth that corrupted affection leads to devastating spiritual consequences, reinforcing the essential call for purity in every dimension of intimacy and expression of love. Our gestures, whether physical or symbolic, must continually reflect the purity and authenticity of our inward spiritual state.

Lust and unbridled reactions diminish and destroy the power inherent in our lips. The compulsion to respond negatively to every criticism or to assert ourselves defensively can lead us down a dark path, damaging our spiritual sensitivity and conscience. If you seek to understand the condition of someone's conscience, listen closely to what their lips release. Curse words and negative speech not only corrupt our words but destroy the lips' sacred power to reflect the true state of our soul and spirit.

THE PALMS OF THE HANDS: THE SACRED GATEWAY OF DIVINE EXCHANGE AND DESTINY

We have unraveled the profound mystery hidden within Judas's betrayal through a kiss, revealing the spiritual implications of corrupted intimacy. Now we journey deeper into another prophetic mystery the palms of the hands. Open your spiritual eyes and discern the profound revelation concerning these sacred instruments.

From ancient days until now, the palms of our hands have been significant gateways in the realm of the spirit. Hands represent divine exchange, prophetic impartation, and the execution of heavenly authority upon the earth. They are vessels, sanctified channels for divine encounters and the transfer of spiritual blessings.

HANDS AS INSTRUMENTS OF COVENANT AND BLESSING

In scripture, hands have always symbolized powerful covenant exchanges and spiritual impartations. The patriarch Jacob demonstrated this prophetic mystery when he laid his hands upon Ephraim and Manasseh:

> *"And Israel stretched out his right hand, and laid it upon Ephraim's head, who was the younger, and his left hand upon Manasseh's head, guiding his hands wittingly; for Manasseh was the firstborn."*
> Genesis 48:14

This action prophetically rearranged destinies, signifying the profound spiritual authority resting upon consecrated palms. Even the Lord Jesus exemplified this divine truth:

> *"And He took them up in His arms, put His hands upon them, and blessed them."*
> Mark 10:16

Understand deeply: through consecrated hands, destinies are prophetically affirmed and spiritual inheritances established.

ELEVEN // MASTERING THE FLOW OF THE SPIRIT

THE PALMS AS GATEWAYS OF HEALING AND MIRACLES

Healing and miracles are often released through the palms of spiritually pure vessels. Scripture clearly instructs believers:

"They shall lay hands on the sick, and they shall recover."
Mark 16:18

Apostle Paul understood this mystery profoundly, as his hands became conduits of divine power and healing:

"And it came to pass, that the father of Publius lay sick of a fever and of a bloody flux: to whom Paul entered in, and prayed, and laid his hands on him, and healed him."
Acts 28:8

However, beloved, we must recognize an essential requirement for purity:

"Who shall ascend into the hill of the Lord? or who shall stand in His holy place?
He that hath clean hands, and a pure heart; who hath not lifted up his soul unto vanity, nor sworn deceitfully."
Psalm 24:3-4

The effectiveness of divine healing through our hands is directly proportional to the purity of our hearts and lives.

HANDS AS INSTRUMENTS OF AUTHORITY AND DOMINION

The palms of our hands symbolize authority and dominion, powerfully illustrated in the account of Moses:

> *"And it came to pass, when Moses held up his hand, that Israel prevailed: and when he let down his hand, Amalek prevailed."*
> Exodus 17:11

In this moment, Moses's hands prophetically dictated the outcome of a nation's battle. The Psalmist further confirms this spiritual truth:

> *"Blessed be the Lord my strength, which teacheth my hands to war, and my fingers to fight."*
> Psalm 144:1

Realize that our palms carry the weight of spiritual authority, crucial in overcoming battles in the unseen realm.

HANDS MARKED BY SACRIFICE

Above all revelations concerning the palms is the profound symbolism of the pierced hands of Jesus Christ, the ultimate act of divine sacrifice and covenant love:

> *"Then saith He to Thomas, Reach hither thy finger, and behold My hands; and reach hither thy hand, and thrust it into My side: and be not faithless, but believing."*
> John 20:27

While Judas's kiss symbolized deception, Christ's pierced hands symbolize truth, redemption, and eternal love. This contrast prophetically reveals two profound spiritual paths one of betrayal and another of redemption.

THE DANGER OF DEFILING THE PALMS

Hear this spiritually: when we engage with idols or touch unclean things, profound defilement begins automatically. When we handle success without acknowledging that the power to obtain wealth comes solely from God, we defile the spiritual portal and authority of our palms. Scripture declares clearly:

> *"But thou shalt remember the Lord thy God: for it is He that giveth thee power to get wealth, that He may establish His covenant."*
> Deuteronomy 8:18

Indeed, God promises that whatever we lay our hands on shall prosper, but what profit is there in gaining material blessings while losing intimacy and fellowship with God? What gain exists in idolizing the very success that God Himself has brought forth through our hands?

Let every believer consecrate their hands anew, recognizing their divine purpose and the profound spiritual impact they possess. Guard the purity of your actions and the intentions of your heart, knowing that through your hands flows the authority and power of heaven itself. This is a prophetic call: keep your palms holy, for they are sacred gateways appointed by God to fulfill His divine purpose.

THE SOLES OF YOUR FEET: POSSESSING TERRITORIES AND ESTABLISHING DOMINION

Having deeply explored the sacred mysteries of the palms of our hands and their profound spiritual implications, we now move forward to yet another vital prophetic gateway: the soles of our feet. Just as the palms of our hands symbolize authority, healing, and divine impartation, the soles of our feet embody God's promise of dominion, possession, and unshakable establishment.

THE POWER TO POSSESS TERRITORIES

From the earliest times, God connected spiritual authority and territorial dominion explicitly to the soles of His servants' feet. This principle is vividly established in Joshua chapter 1:

> *"Every place that the sole of your foot shall tread upon, that have I given unto you, as I said unto Moses."*
> Joshua 1:3

Understand prophetically: wherever your feet step, spiritual transactions take place, releasing divine authority to claim territories and expand God's Kingdom on earth. This spiritual act of possession is not merely symbolic but carries tangible power and heavenly endorsement.

FEET ANCHORED IN UNMOVABLE ESTABLISHMENT

In addition to possession, our feet spiritually represent the stability and permanence of our divine positioning in God. The Psalmist profoundly captures this:

ELEVEN // MASTERING THE FLOW OF THE SPIRIT

"He will not suffer thy foot to be moved: he that keepeth thee will not slumber."
Psalm 121:3

A believer whose feet are established in righteousness and truth is divinely stabilized against shifting circumstances and spiritual opposition. Such individuals become immovable, steadfast, and unwavering, secured firmly in their prophetic destiny.

FEET AS INSTRUMENTS OF VICTORY AND WARFARE

Prophetically, the soles of our feet symbolize dominion and victory over spiritual adversaries. Paul underscores this revelation:

"And the God of peace shall bruise Satan under your feet shortly."
Romans 16:20

This prophetic insight affirms that spiritual victory is not distant but intimately connected to the believer's feet. Through Christ, we have authority to trample upon every power of darkness, firmly establishing God's divine order and peace.

FEET AS MESSENGERS OF PEACE AND GOSPEL PROCLAMATION

The spiritual significance of feet extends beyond territorial conquest and warfare to the powerful proclamation of God's Kingdom. Scripture beautifully proclaims:

"How beautiful upon the mountains are the feet of him that bringeth good tidings, that publisheth peace; that bringeth good

tidings of good, that publisheth salvation."
Isaiah 52:7

Our feet carry the transformative power of the gospel, establishing God's divine presence and ushering in spiritual awakening wherever we tread.

GUARDING THE SACREDNESS OF YOUR FEET

However, just as defilement can affect our hands, our feet must remain spiritually pure and consecrated. The prophetic importance of maintaining purity is clearly illustrated when Moses approached the burning bush:

"And He said, Draw not nigh hither: put off thy shoes from off thy feet, for the place whereon thou standest is holy ground."
Exodus 3:5

Thus, understanding the spiritual significance of the soles of our feet requires careful consecration, ensuring that we walk in holiness, humility, and reverence.

PERSONAL TESTIMONY: REVELATION CHURCH AND UNITED KINGDOM CRUSADE

One evening, as I taught on YouTube, during a short break, I was caught up in a powerful vision. Father Abraham appeared and declared, *"My son, not everyone has been given the grace to build God a temple on earth. You are among the few anointed by heaven for this sacred assignment."* He instructed me clearly: once we found the land destined for our church, I was to remove my shoes, walk upon it, and declare, *"This shall be God's house, and many souls shall be saved unto the glory of God the Father,*

ELEVEN // MASTERING THE FLOW OF THE SPIRIT

the Son, and the Holy Spirit."

Despite the fear surrounding physical gatherings during COVID-19, we obeyed this divine instruction. When we found the building, costing over eight million dollars, we had no resources. Yet, within less than one month after following these prophetic instructions declaring God's word and praying over the land the necessary funds miraculously manifested.

Similarly, when God sent me to the UK for a crusade, pastors discouraged me, warning of difficulties in breaking spiritual ground in Europe. Yet, as I fasted, prayed, and prophetically walked the venue grounds, over five thousand souls gathered, bearing witness to the power of obedience and prophetic action in claiming spiritual territory for the Kingdom.

Beloved, the soles of your feet are sacred gateways, instruments of divine possession, unmovable establishment, spiritual victory, and powerful proclamation. Recognize the authority vested in you by heaven to claim territories, remain immovable in God's purposes, and carry forth the message of peace and salvation. Consecrate your footsteps, for in every step taken in holiness lies the divine promise of Kingdom advancement and spiritual dominion.

A HOUSE OR A TEMPLE?

When we gain revelation regarding the significance of our divine instruments the members of our bodies a profound clarity settles upon us. This particular truth I will share with you was imparted to me directly by the angel assigned to my life by the Lord Jesus Himself.

One day, having just finished showering and beginning to dress,

I suddenly felt the overwhelming presence of the Holy Spirit enveloping the room. Immediately, I recognized that God was about to communicate divine instructions. Still undressed, I turned and saw clearly the angel of the Lord standing before me. He began to speak, delivering a crucial revelation.

> *"There are two kinds of believers," he explained, "some have become temples, and others remain merely houses."* He elaborated further, *"Many believe that simply abstaining from unclean things makes one useful to God. While purity and abstaining from sin are necessary, they alone are insufficient. God is seeking true consecration a complete surrender of every aspect of your being. Consecration means more than avoiding wrongdoing; it means handing the reins fully to God, allowing Him to govern every area of your life."*

> *He then reminded me of the teachings of our Lord Jesus, specifically the parable where a demon, cast out of a person, roams dry places and then returns with seven spirits more wicked than itself. Finding the house clean and orderly, they re-enter, worsening the person's state beyond its original condition.*

> *"When the unclean spirit is gone out of a man, he walketh through dry places, seeking rest, and findeth none.*
> *Then he saith, I will return into my house from whence I came out; and when he is come, he findeth it empty, swept, and garnished.*
> *Then goeth he, and taketh with himself seven other spirits more wicked than himself, and they enter in and dwell there: and the last state of that man is worse than the first. Even so shall it be also unto this wicked generation."*
> Matthew 12:43-45

ELEVEN // MASTERING THE FLOW OF THE SPIRIT

The angel then posed a critical question: "If the house was clean, how could the demons re-enter?" He provided clarity on this mystery, explaining, "A clean house alone does not deter demonic entities, for cleanliness by itself does not guarantee God's indwelling presence. A house still signifies human ownership and control a place where man determines activities and outcomes. Despite our best efforts, a mere house though clean remains inadequate for divine habitation, for Yahweh does not dwell in structures built solely by human hands or maintained by human strength. God dwells exclusively in that which He has chosen, sanctified, and consecrated through the blood of the Lamb."

The angel emphasized, "The Lord Jesus never referred to His own body as a house but rather as a temple. His body was a temple fully consecrated to God the Father, the dwelling place of the fullness of the Godhead. "For in Him dwelleth all the fulness of the Godhead bodily" (Colossians 2:9). Similarly, the apostles instructed believers to recognize their bodies not merely as houses but as temples God's sacred habitation. Scripture declares, "…Greater is He that is in you than he that is in the world" (1 John 4:4), underscoring the truth that someone far greater than ourselves must reside within us."

The Apostle Paul clearly taught this principle, saying:

"Know ye not that ye are the temple of God, and that the Spirit of God dwelleth in you?"
1 Corinthians 3:16

Every place that God has designated as His dwelling has always been fully consecrated and dedicated by sacrifice, just as Solomon consecrated the temple.

"And king Solomon offered a sacrifice of twenty and two thousand oxen, and an hundred and twenty thousand sheep: so the king and all the people dedicated the house of God."
2 Chronicles 7:5

For us as believers, Jesus Christ Himself is the ultimate and perfect sacrifice. Therefore, our sacrifice now involves living wholly surrendered to Him, presenting our bodies as living sacrifices.

"I beseech you therefore, brethren, by the mercies of God, that ye present your bodies a living sacrifice, holy, acceptable unto God, which is your reasonable service."
Romans 12:1

Only then can our Holy God freely utilize us without restriction. Even in moments of weakness and sin, we rise again not through self-righteousness, which scripture describes as filthy rags:

"But we are all as an unclean thing, and all our righteousnesses are as filthy rags; and we all do fade as a leaf; and our iniquities, like the wind, have taken us away."
Isaiah 64:6

We can get back up from our failures by relying wholly upon the righteousness of our King, who paid the highest price for our redemption.

Further exploration of this crucial revelation will be shared in the forthcoming book that the Lord commanded me to write, entitled "The Consecration of the Prophet." The core message remains: unless we offer ourselves entirely to the Lord in complete consecration, yielding every aspect to His sovereign will, we will produce nothing of

ELEVEN // MASTERING THE FLOW OF THE SPIRIT

eternal value, and our bodily members will be indistinguishable from those of ordinary mortal men. Consecration alone transforms us from mere houses into temples, sanctified and empowered by God's divine presence.

Twelve
SERVING ANOTHER'S VISION

TWELVE // SERVING ANOTHER'S VISION

One of the most overlooked keys to prophetic growth and divine promotion is the ability to serve another man's vision. In a generation driven by platforms, personal brands, and self-made ministry empires, many have lost sight of the simple but profound truth: ministry is not about building our name, it's about building God's will. True ministry, and especially prophetic ministry, is not about serving your own ambition, but aligning yourself with God's agenda, even when it means laying your own dreams aside.

MANY ARE ANOINTED, BUT FOR WHOSE VISION?

There are many in the Church today, whether they be pastors, prophets, bishops, who began with genuine anointing, but have drifted from Heaven's assignment. They are caught up in status, applause, church expansion, and material gain, forgetting the very reason they were anointed in the first place.

The mark of prophetic immaturity is, "I want to be known," whereas the mark of prophetic maturity is, "I want Him to be known." God never anoints for entertainment or ego; He only anoints for His mission.

THE EXAMPLE OF THE LORD JESUS CHRIST

Our greatest example is the Lord Jesus Himself. He was God in the flesh, yet fully submitted to the Father.

"O my Father, if it be possible, let this cup pass from Me:

> *nevertheless not as I will, but as Thou wilt."*
> Matthew 26:39

Here, we see the Savior of the world wrestling with the weight of His assignment. He had emotions, He felt fear, anguish, and sorrow. But even in the agony of Gethsemane, He chose His Father's will over His own. This is the highest form of prophetic alignment: total surrender to a vision greater than your feelings.

> *"And He said unto them, How is it that ye sought Me? wist ye not that I must be about My Father's business?"*
> Luke 2:49

Even as a child, Jesus understood: His life was not His own. He didn't pursue personal gain. He pursued the fulfillment of His Father's desires.

> *"Then answered Jesus and said unto them, Verily, verily, I say unto you, The Son can do nothing of Himself, but what He seeth the Father do: for what things soever He doeth, these also doeth the Son likewise."*
> John 5:19

This is submission in its purest form. Jesus did not move, speak, or act outside of His Father's activity. He functioned in perfect prophetic obedience, not because He lacked power, but because He chose honor and alignment over independence, even while being equal with God.

> *"Who, being in the form of God, thought it not robbery to be equal with God:*
> *But made Himself of no reputation, and took upon Him the form*

TWELVE // SERVING ANOTHER'S VISION

of a servant, and was made in the likeness of men:
And being found in fashion as a man, He humbled Himself, and
became obedient unto death, even the death of the cross."
Philippians 2:6-8

Though equal with God, Jesus humbled Himself, becoming obedient unto death. Because of His humility and service, God highly exalted Him. This is the mystery: Submission precedes exaltation.

GOD HONORS SERVANTS BEFORE HE ELEVATES GENERALS

You cannot be trusted with your own vision until you've proven faithful with another's. Serving another's vision tests your heart, your motives, your discipline, and your humility. It purifies your intentions. It teaches you the heartbeat of God.

"If ye have not been faithful in that which is another man's, who
shall give you that which is your own?"
Luke 16:12

Serving another's vision is not punishment but preparation.

- Joshua served Moses before leading Israel.
- Elisha served Elijah before receiving the double portion.
- Timothy served Paul before pastoring churches.
- Jesus served the Father to redeem the world.

If you truly want to walk in the prophetic and see God use you with power and precision, learn to serve someone else's vision without entitlement. Let the cry of your heart be, *"Not my will, but Thine be done."* When you align with Heaven's order, God will trust you with His glory.

HOW TO SERVE ANOTHER'S VISION: KEYS TO LOYALTY, EXCELLENCE, AND ALIGNMENT IN THE PROPHETIC

Serving another's vision is not about limitation; it is the pathway to divine promotion. It is the school of the Spirit where God tests your capacity, your heart, and your readiness for responsibility.

Here are the practical dimensions of what it truly means to serve another's vision:

1. SERVE WITH LOYALTY EVEN WHEN IT'S NOT CONVENIENT

Loyalty is not about agreement, it's about alignment. True sons and servants remain consistent even when it's uncomfortable. They don't abandon their post when corrected, overlooked, or challenged.

"A friend loveth at all times, and a brother is born for adversity."
Proverbs 17:17

Loyalty means:
- You cover, not expose;
- You protect, not compete;
- You remain faithful, not only when you're celebrated, but also when you're tested.

Ask yourself: Can God trust me to serve another's vision without demanding my own platform?

2. SERVE WITH EXCELLENCE AS UNTO THE LORD

Excellence is not perfection. Excellence is doing your best with a heart of worship. Whether you're setting up chairs or carrying your leader's Bible, do it with the same intensity as if you were preaching to millions.

"And whatsoever ye do, do it heartily, as to the Lord, and not unto men."
Colossians 3:23

Excellence means:
- You anticipate needs before being asked;
- You don't need to be watched to be faithful;
- You don't do the bare minimum, because you go above and beyond.

Excellence attracts impartation.

3. SERVE WITH ALIGNMENT UNDERSTAND THE VISION, NOT JUST THE PERSON

It's not enough to love the leader; you must understand the burden they carry. When you serve a vision, you must carry it like it's your own. Learn to feel what they feel, protect what they protect, and pursue what they pursue.

"And the LORD answered me, and said, Write the vision, and make it plain upon tables, that he may run that readeth it."
Habakkuk 2:2

Alignment means:
- You don't pull the ministry in a different direction;
- You speak the same language as your leader;
- You replicate their heart, not just their actions.

You are not there to create division; you are there to advance the assignment.

4. SERVE IN SILENCE
NOT EVERYTHING NEEDS TO BE ANNOUNCED

Some of the most powerful seasons of your life will be invisible to the crowd but seen by God. When David served Saul, he played the harp in private long before he killed Goliath in public. He didn't need to be announced. On the contrary; he needed to be faithful.

"That thine alms may be in secret: and thy Father which seeth in secret Himself shall reward thee openly."
Matthew 6:4

Silence means:
- You don't need public recognition to be faithful;
- You let God announce you when the time is right;
- You trust the process without self-promotion.

TWELVE // SERVING ANOTHER'S VISION

5. **SERVE WITH DISCERNMENT**
   KNOW WHEN TO MOVE AND WHEN TO WAIT

Timing is everything. Elisha didn't demand the mantle; he waited until Elijah was taken. Gehazi moved without discernment and inherited a curse. Not every opportunity is divine. Stay planted until God, and your leader, releases you.

"To everything there is a season, and a time to every purpose under the heaven."
Ecclesiastes 3:1

Discernment means:
- You don't rush out of alignment prematurely;
- You recognize seasons of training, not just seasons of elevation;
- You stay until the assignment is complete.

6. **SERVE WITH INTEGRITY**
   WHEN NO ONE IS WATCHING

What you do when no one is watching determines what Heaven releases when everyone is watching. God watches how you serve privately before He trusts you publicly.

"He that is faithful in that which is least is faithful also in much: and he that is unjust in the least is unjust also in much."
Luke 16:10

Integrity means:
- You show up when it's hard;

- You honor your leader even when you're offended;
- You do the right thing even when it costs you.

A CHARGE TO SERVE FAITHFULLY

When you are serving another's vision, you are not merely helping a person; you are helping God's agenda *through* that person. Serving in this way is how God matures your heart, shapes your character, and prepares you for your own divine assignment. When you serve with loyalty, excellence, and alignment, God Himself will lift you. You won't need to announce yourself because He will do it.

> *"Humble yourselves therefore under the mighty hand of God, that He may exalt you in due time."*
> 1 Peter 5:6

TWELVE // SERVING ANOTHER'S VISION

A Prayer for Those Serving or Waiting for Release into Their Assignment

Father, I lift up your people: those who have sacrificed everything to follow You, those who are serving faithfully in hidden places, and those who are waiting patiently for the day of their release.

Lord, may Your presence be their strength and Your promise their anchor. Give them the assurance that their labor is not in vain. Let them know deep within that the fruit will come, because Your Word remains true and what You promise will surely manifest in due time.

My God, strengthen their hearts. Let them not move ahead of You, but teach them to walk with You, just as the children of Israel followed the cloud by day and the pillar of fire by night. Let their steps be ordered by Your Spirit.

Remind them, Holy Spirit, to walk in humility, and to resist the desire for self-glory or premature elevation. Make them bondservants of Your vision, not their own. Let their hearts burn for Your will above all else.

Keep them, Father, from wrong counsel through the voices that tempt them to abort their divine assignment in pursuit of personal fame or vanity. Surround them with wisdom, with godly mentors, and with the fear of the Lord.

Give them a new heart, a servant's heart. The same heart that was in You, Lord Jesus, when You walked the earth in full submission to the Father. Let them find joy in obedience, peace in the process, and honor in servanthood.

Lord, supply all their needs, spiritual, emotional and

physical, so they do not faint in the wilderness. Let them not trade their birthright for momentary relief, as Esau did. Keep their vision clear and their faith strong.

I declare: they will finish well. They will be released in Your time, with Your favor, and in Your power.

In the name of Jesus Christ, Amen.

Thirteen
DEFILED VESSELS

THIRTEEN // DEFILED VESSELS

"A man's pride shall bring him low: but honour shall uphold the humble in spirit."
Proverbs 29:23

This verse is a prophetic key: it unveils the spiritual law that governs both exaltation and downfall. Pride doesn't just corrupt behavior; it affects the very core of a person. It reaches into the spirit and soul, defiling the internal senses, particularly the *ears and eyes of the spirit*, which are essential for prophetic function. Pride makes the spirit dull, heavy, and insensitive, rendering a person of *no prophetic use* in the hands of the Holy Spirit.

When pride is active, it disconnects man from divine flow and spiritual perception. It renders him carnal, earthbound, and void of revelation. A proud heart becomes barbaric toward the voice of God; it is brutish, resistant, and unaware of His ways. Pride does not just puff a person up; it sets them up for a divine dismantling.

Let's examine three key words from the verse in their original Hebrew, which unlock a fuller understanding:

1. LOW (SHÂPHÊL)

This word means to be brought down, debased, or humiliated. It speaks of being stripped of value, significance, or spiritual stature. Pride always results in a lowering, not just of position, but of prophetic perception and divine favor.

2. HUMBLE (SHÂPHÂL)

Interestingly, this word comes from the same root as *low*, yet in this context, it carries a voluntary posture. It is not a forced humiliation, but a chosen position of surrender. A humble person lowers themselves before God, and in doing so, they become a candidate for divine use and spiritual clarity.

3. UPHOLD (TÂMAK)

This word means to sustain, to hold up, to retain. It is God's response to humility. God doesn't just lift the humble; He sustains them. He makes them steady, consistent, and able to carry honor without it corrupting their soul. To be upheld is to be preserved by the strength of God Himself.

When we consider these three things, the principle is this: pride pulls down, humility positions, and God's honor sustains. One path ends in spiritual dullness and divine resistance. The other leads to sustained favor, clarity, and usefulness in the hands of the Spirit.

Our precious ancestors are a sobering example of how the sin of pride leads to the disconnection of prophetic insight and the descent into total carnality. Through their fall, we witness a spiritual unraveling, a gradual loss of divine sensitivity that began with disobedience and ended in exile.

Observe how their spiritual senses diminished. In the beginning, they walked with God, communed with Him in the cool of the day. They could see Him, hear Him, perceive His movements and discern His voice with clarity. But the moment pride entered through the desire to be "like God," independent of His instruction, their prophetic faculties began to collapse.

Their spiritual sight was the first to go. Their eyes were no longer filled with light, but with shame. They saw themselves through the lens of guilt, not glory. Their nakedness was not only physically; spiritually they were exposed, vulnerable, and disconnected. Their ability to hear was all that remained, but even that got strained. When God called to them, *"Where are you?"* they no longer ran to His voice;

THIRTEEN // DEFILED VESSELS

they hid from it. The ears that once delighted in His presence now recoiled in fear and condemnation.

This pattern reveals a tragic principle: when pride enters, the senses of the spirit begin to shut down. Sight is clouded and hearing becomes distorted. The inner man begins to live by the flesh, not by revelation. What was once communion becomes confusion. What was once intimacy becomes distance. Soon, even the last remaining sense, hearing, is lost. The voice of God, which once echoed clearly in the garden, became faint in the world. The prophetic frequency became rare, and generations were born into spiritual deafness.

This is the price of pride: it blinds, it numbs, it deafens, and ultimately, it disconnects. It turns divine image-bearers into spiritual barbarians, aware only of the natural, and estranged from the supernatural. Unless intercepted by grace, that disconnection becomes generational.

The decline that began in the garden did not end there. It reverberates through time and can still be seen clearly in the condition of the modern Church. Just as our ancestors gradually lost their spiritual senses due to pride and disobedience, so too has much of the present-day Church drifted into a similar state: disconnected from the prophetic, suspicious of the supernatural, and increasingly governed by logic, form, and tradition rather than by revelation and divine encounter.

The prophetic, which was once central to God's relationship with His people, has become, in many places, optional, misunderstood, or even despised. The voice of God is treated as something rare or extreme, reserved only for the "elite" or dismissed entirely as emotionalism or manipulation. This is the same pattern seen in the garden: when pride enters, perception closes.

Many churches today operate with form but lack fire. They are filled with structure but void of sensitivity. Programs have replaced presence. Theology has replaced intimacy. Knowledge about God has taken precedence over encounters *with* God, and the prophetic, God's method of revealing His mind and will, is often labeled as excessive, divisive, or irrelevant.

Like Adam and Eve after the fall, the Church still *hears* sermons, songs, and teachings, but many no longer *recognize* the true voice of the Spirit. The sound of Heaven has been drowned out by the noise of culture, intellect, and tradition. There is a hearing, but no discerning. A gathering, but no transformation.

Pride manifests in subtle ways:

- A refusal to yield to the Spirit's movement.
- A resistance to correction through prophetic voices.
- A trust in human systems over supernatural solutions.
- A reliance on polished speech rather than anointed utterance.

This is why we see churches that are full in attendance but empty in impact. They are blind to what God is doing in this generation, deaf to His warnings, numb to His presence, and suspicious of His power. Just as in Eden, when pride and independence crept in, spiritual sensitivity declined, the same is true today.

But praise be to God, there is a remnant rising. Those who are hungry not just for church, but for God. Those who refuse to despise the prophetic and who welcome the supernatural. Those who humble themselves enough to say, *"Speak, Lord, for Your servant hears."*

THIRTEEN // DEFILED VESSELS

EFFECTS OF BEING DEFILED BY PRIDE

When men can no longer hear from God, they begin to seek other sources. This is the tragedy we are witnessing in much of the world and even in parts of the Church today. Many believers don't realize that things like witchcraft, sorcery, and divination are not truly supernatural but rather super-carnal. These practices are not born of Heaven, but of the fallen flesh, rebellion, and demonic influence. The root of it all is pride.

Pride separates a person from the presence and voice of God. It corrupts the spiritual senses, blinding the eyes of the spirit, dulling the ears, and numbing the heart. When pride enters, a person becomes carnal, disconnected, and spiritually deaf. And once they can no longer hear from God, they will start reaching for anything that looks or sounds spiritual, even if it comes from darkness.

This is what happened to Satan himself. He was once an anointed cherub, a glorious being in Heaven (Ezekiel 28:14-15). When pride was found in him, he fell. God cast him out of His presence. By the time we get to Isaiah 14, he is no longer seen as glorious, but mocked as a mere man:

> *"They that see thee shall narrowly look upon thee, and consider thee, saying, Is this the man that made the earth to tremble, that did shake kingdoms?"*
> Isaiah 14:16

This verse reveals a powerful truth: pride demotes the spiritual to the carnal. Even Satan, once radiant with glory, became stripped of divine value and reduced to shame. The same thing happens to anyone who follows his path.

"Now the works of the flesh are manifest, which are these;

> *Adultery, fornication, uncleanness, lasciviousness,*
> *Idolatry, witchcraft, hatred, variance, emulations, wrath, strife, seditions, heresies,*
> *Envyings, murders, drunkenness, revellings, and such like..."*
> Galatians 5:19-21

Apostle Paul in Galatians tells us plainly that witchcraft and sorcery are works of the flesh, not works of the Spirit. They are rooted in the desire to control, to manipulate, or to gain hidden knowledge apart from God. This is why 1 Samuel 15:23 says, *"...rebellion is as the sin of witchcraft, and stubbornness is as iniquity and idolatry."*

When people no longer want to hear God's voice, or when they've lost the ability to, pride leads them to seek out counterfeits. This is exactly what happened to King Saul. After rejecting God's command, the Lord stopped speaking to him. Instead of repenting he sought out a witch, and that decision sealed his downfall.

> *"Then said Saul unto his servants, Seek me a woman that hath a familiar spirit, that I may go to her, and enquire of her. And his servants said to him, Behold, there is a woman that hath a familiar spirit at Endor."*
> 1 Samuel 28:7

This is the danger of spiritual deafness: it opens the door to deception. When people are spiritually deaf, they reach out for false voices, false visions, and dark revelations that promise insight but lead to destruction.

The good news is this: God still speaks, and He draws near to the humble.

> *"Though the Lord be high, yet hath He respect unto the lowly: but*

THIRTEEN // DEFILED VESSELS

the proud He knoweth afar off."
Psalm 138:6

God is close to those who bow low. He honors those who walk in humility, and He opens their spiritual ears to hear His voice.

The only cure for spiritual deafness is to return to God with a sincere and humble heart. While He has never stopped speaking, He waits to be sought.

"And ye shall seek Me, and find Me, when ye shall search for Me with all your heart."
Jeremiah 29:13

When David fell into sin and felt the silence of God, he didn't run to darkness. David ran to the Lord because he understood that true restoration can only come from God, and thus he cried out:

"Restore unto me the joy of Thy salvation; and uphold me with Thy free Spirit."
Psalm 51:12

Saul's story on the other hand is a solemn warning. Instead of repenting, he turned to a witch for answers, a choice that pulled him even further from God's presence. When we ignore the voice of the Lord and seek answers from elsewhere, we do not just drift, we depart. We break alignment with the One who gives life.

"For thou shalt worship no other god: for the Lord, whose name is Jealous, is a jealous God."
Exodus 34:14

God desires our full attention. He is not silent without reason;

He is waiting for hearts that will return. That is why the prophet asked,

> *"And when they shall say unto you, Seek unto them that have familiar spirits, and unto wizards that peep, and that mutter: should not a people seek unto their God? for the living to the dead?"*
> Isaiah 8:19

The answer is eternal and unchanging: yes. We were created to seek Him, to hear Him, and to live by every word that proceeds from His mouth. Every other voice is a counterfeit, and all counterfeits lead to confusion, not communion.

THIRTEEN // DEFILED VESSELS

Prayer of Renunciation, Repentance, and Restoration

If you have ever been involved in the occult, witchcraft, sorcery, divination, white magic, black magic, voodoo, or any form of dark arts, I urge you to pray this prayer with faith and humility, and to pray it out loud. This is not a silent prayer. Let both Heaven and Hell hear your voice as you step into the light of truth and freedom.

<u>Please make sure to pray this in a safe and private place and not while driving or distracted.</u> This is important, as there may be demonic manifestations during or after the prayer. These spirits will be confronted and driven out, and your full attention and spiritual focus is needed as the power of God works in and through you.

Father, in the name of Jesus Christ, I come before You with a heart bowed in humility. I acknowledge that I have walked in darkness, knowingly or unknowingly, and today I ask for Your mercy. I thank You for drawing me to this moment. By Your grace, You have opened my eyes to the truth. It is not by accident that I have found these words. It is Your love that has reached for me.

Father, I believe You love me. *You proved Your love by giving Your only begotten Son, Jesus Christ, to die for my sins and rise again for my freedom. I confess that I have participated in things that grieve Your Spirit, such as witchcraft, sorcery, divination, magic, and the occult. But today, I make a decision to turn away from every dark path and return fully to You.*

By the power of the blood of Jesus Christ of

Nazareth, *I renounce, reject, and break every covenant, agreement, or attachment I have made with Satan, demons, familiar spirits, or any force of darkness, whether knowingly or unknowingly. Let every legal right of the enemy over my life be revoked now, in the name of Jesus.*

I declare that I am no longer bound to darkness. I am no longer tied to the lies or illusions of the enemy. I belong to Jesus Christ, and through Him I am made clean.

Father, wash me. Purify me. Deliver me. *Let every chain of bondage be broken off my spirit, soul, and body. Let the fire of the Holy Ghost consume every residue of the enemy in my life. Let Your blood speak a better word over me, cleansing, redeeming, and restoring me into full fellowship with You.*

Holy Spirit, fill me afresh. *Fill every empty place. Restore what was broken. Heal what was wounded. Teach me to walk in truth, in righteousness, and in Your presence daily. I surrender completely to You.*

Thank You, Father, for hearing my prayer. Thank You for forgiving me, restoring me, and calling me Your own. From this day forward, I declare that I am a child of Light, and I will never go back.

In Jesus' mighty name, Amen.

Fourteen
PROPHETIC DEPTH

FOURTEEN // PROPHETIC DEPTH

One of the most frequent questions I encounter from believers is, "How can I become accurate in the prophetic?" This genuine desire has unintentionally caused many who are authentically called into prophetic ministry to become spiritually stagnant. Such stagnation typically results from seeking shortcuts or formulas to obtain something that God has freely provided to all believers. Tragically, some even quench the Spirit, refusing to speak unless their expressions mirror their favorite prophets. Others abandon their divine call entirely due to an excessive focus on achieving prophetic accuracy. This reveals a fundamental misunderstanding of how God truly operates.

The accuracy we must pursue is accurately representing the Word the Lord has spoken. While specific details and revelations are beautiful and impactful, they hold no true value apart from authentically expressing the Master's voice and intent.

Prophetic accuracy does not depend on the measure or magnitude of one's gift. Spiritual gifts themselves do not expand; rather, it is our spiritual maturity and sensitivity that develop over time. Through intimate fellowship with God and faithful submission to His Spirit, we refine our ability to minister effectively, mastering sensitivity to the divine flow and yielding confidently as the Holy Spirit speaks through us.

THE SPIRITUAL REALM, EYES & LIGHT

Genesis 1 and John 1 convey the same spiritual truths from two complementary perspectives, each enhancing our understanding of spiritual realities. Contrary to popular belief, the spiritual realm is inherently dark. In Scripture, "darkness" (Hebrew: *choshek* – חֹשֶׁךְ) can symbolize evil, represent hidden or unknown things, or simply reflect the absence of light.

Let us take a look at this verse in 1 John chapter 1:

"This then is the message which we have heard of Him, and declare unto you, that God is light, and in Him is no darkness at all."
1 John 1:5

This verse reveals God as pure, illuminating light. Yet, in 1 Kings chapter 8 it states:

"Then spake Solomon, The LORD said that He would dwell in the thick darkness."
1 Kings 8:12

How can God be both light and dwell in darkness? This apparent paradox is resolved through symbolic understanding. The Greek word for "light" (*phos* – φῶς) signifies purity, revelation, and holiness. Conversely, the Hebrew term for "thick darkness" (*araphel* – עֲרָפֶל) points to God's hiddenness and majesty, elements of His essence beyond human comprehension. This darkness is not evil but protects the sacredness of His divine presence.

Prophetic depth requires spiritual perception, and genuine perception needs light. The inherent darkness of the spiritual realm makes discerning God's presence challenging. Unlocking these mysteries involves the entrance of God's Word into our spirit.

"The entrance of thy words giveth light; it giveth understanding unto the simple."
Psalm 119:130

The Hebrew word for "entrance," פֶּתַח (petach), means "opening" or "unfolding," indicating spiritual illumination occurs as

FOURTEEN // PROPHETIC DEPTH

God's Word penetrates our spirits. This spiritual truth mirrors physical sight. The eye needs external light to perceive clearly. Light enters through the cornea, pupil, and lens before reaching the retina, translating into signals interpreted by the brain as vision. Similarly, without internal illumination from God's Word, spiritual eyes remain blind to divine mysteries.

BIBLICAL CASE STUDY: ELISHA AND GEHAZI

In 2 Kings chapter 6, Elisha and his servant were surrounded by enemy forces. The servant, overwhelmed by natural sight, feared greatly. Then, Elisha prayed.

> *"And when the servant of the man of God was risen early, and gone forth, behold, an host compassed the city both with horses and chariots. And his servant said unto him, Alas, my master! how shall we do?*
> *And he answered, Fear not: for they that be with us are more than they that be with them.*
> *And Elisha prayed, and said, LORD, I pray thee, open his eyes, that he may see. And the LORD opened the eyes of the young man; and he saw: and, behold, the mountain was full of horses and chariots of fire round about Elisha."*
> 2 Kings 6:15-17

This demonstrates spiritual sight transcending physical perception to bring clarity amidst uncertainty. However, Elisha's servant could not sustain this elevated spiritual sight, lacking deep roots in God's Word. While Elisha knew he was protected without visible confirmation, his servant needed physical evidence. Similarly, in the previous chapter, Gehazi's attempt to deceive Elisha (2 Kings 5:25-27) revealed his shallow spiritual foundation, resulting in leprosy. This illustrates that supernatural experiences alone are insufficient without God's Word deeply embedded within one's heart.

PRACTICAL WAYS TO INCREASE SPIRITUAL LIGHT

1. **CONSISTENT MEDITATION ON SCRIPTURE**
   Regularly meditate on God's Word, allowing revelation to unfold.

2. **PRAYING FOR REVELATION**
   Pray intentionally for spiritual sight and sensitivity to the Holy Spirit.

3. **JOURNALING DIVINE INSIGHTS**
   Document insights and revelations to reinforce spiritual truths.

4. **APPLYING GOD'S WORD**
   Actively practice Scriptural truths, deepening your spiritual understanding.

5. **ACCOUNTABILITY AND FELLOWSHIP**
   Engage with spiritually mature believers for guidance, correction, and encouragement.

True prophetic depth is carefully cultivated, not rushed. It is developed steadily through encounters with God's Word and patiently embracing His profound, unfolding mysteries.

Fifteen
FEAR IN THE PROPHETIC

FIFTEEN // FEAR IN THE PROPHETIC

Fear in the prophetic ministry is entirely natural. In fact, I personally experience fear each time before ministering. I am acutely aware that without God's divine assistance, my efforts will inevitably fail. Through experience, I've come to profoundly understand that the grace of God is indeed mankind's greatest ally.

Saint Joseph the Hesychast, a revered elder in the Orthodox Church, insightfully expressed:

> *"When grace comes to man, it makes him god. But when it departs from him, then he is ready to fall into every heresy, every delusion, every moral deviation, and even damnation. Everything is supported by the grace of God. But grace also has its requirements before it will dwell in man. It seeks his good intentions, his willpower, and his struggle. Together with grace, man becomes an angel. Without grace, he deviates and becomes a demon."*

This truth vividly captures the essence of prophetic ministry. A godly fear, grounded in reverence and humility, serves as a critical safeguard, ensuring we represent God's heart and voice with utmost accuracy and reverence.

In contrast, the spirit of fear introduced by the enemy scatters our minds with doubts and anxiety, wrongly convincing us that God is unreliable. This demonic fear erodes our confidence in God's unfailing love and empowerment. The Apostle Paul addresses this explicitly in 2 Timothy:

> *"For God hath not given us the spirit of fear; but of power, and of love, and of a sound mind.*
> *Be not thou therefore ashamed of the testimony of our Lord, nor of me his prisoner: but be thou partaker of the afflictions of the gospel according to the power of God;*
> *Who hath saved us, and called us with an holy calling, not*

according to our works, but according to his own purpose and grace, which was given us in Christ Jesus before the world began."
2 Timothy 1:7-9

Paul highlights three essential divine elements that counteract the spirit of fear:

1. **POWER** (δύναμις – DUNAMIS)

Divine empowerment enabling boldness and supernatural effectiveness.

2. **LOVE** (ἀγάπη – AGAPE)

Unconditional divine love, casting out fear and securing us in God's faithful intentions.

3. **A SOUND MIND** (σωφρονισμός – SOPHRONISMOS)

Clarity, disciplined thinking, and balanced judgment essential for prophetic discernment.

Operating within these divine provisions fortifies us against fear, ensuring that our prophetic ministry is characterized by divine authority, accuracy, and effectiveness.

FIFTEEN // FEAR IN THE PROPHETIC

THE FEAR OF MAN

One significant fear we must confront is the fear of man. This fear has hindered many who were destined by God for great purposes. Scripture provides clear guidance to overcome this fear, exemplified vividly in the life of Prophet Jeremiah.

Jeremiah was young and inexperienced when God called him. God addressed his fears explicitly:

> *"Then the word of the Lord came unto me, saying,*
> *Before I formed thee in the belly I knew thee; and before thou camest forth out of the womb I sanctified thee, and I ordained thee a prophet unto the nations.*
> *Then said I, Ah, Lord God! behold, I cannot speak: for I am a child.*
> *But the Lord said unto me, Say not, I am a child: for thou shalt go to all that I shall send thee, and whatsoever I command thee thou shalt speak.*
> *Be not afraid of their faces: for I am with thee to deliver thee, saith the Lord."*
> Jeremiah 1:4-8

God instructed Jeremiah to embrace boldness without arrogance, affirming:

> *"Thou therefore gird up thy loins, and arise, and speak unto them all that I command thee: be not dismayed at their faces, lest I confound thee before them."*
> Jeremiah 1:17

Boldness, however, must never be mistaken for rudeness. The prophetic word must always be shared with humility and compassion, respecting the dignity of all people. Proverbs 18 aptly reminds us:

> *"Before destruction the heart of man is haughty, and before honour is humility."*
> Proverbs 18:12

THE FEAR OF BEING WRONG

Prophetic ministry is fundamentally about God and His immeasurable love for humanity. It is not about our personal reputations or accuracy. We are vessels, servants delivering His word. It is God alone who determines the outcome and fulfillment of His message.

Many prophetic voices have become paralyzed by the fear of being wrong, mistakenly carrying burdens that belong solely to God. Our pride and self-concern must diminish completely, enabling God to freely speak through us. As the Scripture declares:

> *"So shall my word be that goeth forth out of my mouth: it shall not return unto me void."*
> Isaiah 55:11

Yet, for this truth to manifest fully in our ministries, we must embody the humility expressed in the gospel of John:

> *"He must increase, but I must decrease."*
> John 3:30

FIFTEEN // FEAR IN THE PROPHETIC

THE FEAR OF MISTAKES

Interestingly, one of the greatest teachers in the prophetic journey is our mistakes. Mistakes genuinely serve as gateways to understanding God's heart more deeply because maturity requires instruction, and instructions are profoundly valued when learned through error. Consider how through sin, humanity discovered the profound depths of God's love. Through failing in God's sight, humanity gained the capacity to understand and receive His immense, eternal love, a love surpassing our finite comprehension. As the Scriptures say:

> *"For God so loved the world, that He gave His only begotten Son, that whosoever believeth in Him should not perish, but have everlasting life."*
> John 3:16

Without Adam and Eve's transgression, we would never have had the room or capacity within ourselves to truly comprehend and receive the magnitude of God's love.

Embracing our mistakes with humility allows us to experience profound spiritual growth and deep intimacy with God. When we develop the courage and humility to acknowledge and accept our prophetic and life mistakes openly, though the world may look down upon us, God Almighty will elevate us even higher in prophetic authority and spiritual maturity. From personal experience, I have discovered that God sometimes allows mistakes as a test, observing whether we possess a genuinely repentant heart that is ready and willing to be molded by His corrective grace.

CLARIFYING COMMON MISCONCEPTIONS

Prophets are not God; only God is omniscient and infallible. Prophets receive revelation in part.

> *"For we know in part, and we prophesy in part."*
> 1 Corinthians 13:9

Recognizing this truth helps both prophetic messengers and recipients approach prophecy with humility and openness to God's continual guidance. Often people approach me assuming, "Prophet, you already know what's happening," but I must consistently remind them, with humility and reverence, that I am not God and do not know everything. Acts 17:11 encourages believers to search the scriptures diligently, emphasizing that prophetic revelation must align with God's Word. Embracing this truth frees us from unrealistic expectations and positions us to be more authentic and effective in our prophetic service.

GUIDELINES FOR DISCERNMENT

Effective prophetic discernment requires intentional cultivation. Regular communion with God through prayer, fasting, and meditating on His Word sharpens our spiritual sensitivity. We are reminded in Hebrews chapter 4:

> *"For the word of God is quick, and powerful, and sharper than any twoedged sword, piercing even to the dividing asunder of soul and spirit, and of the joints and marrow, and is a discerner of the*

thoughts and intents of the heart."
Hebrews 4:12

Consistently aligning ourselves with scripture and submitting prophetic words to trusted spiritual counsel are vital practices that ensure accurate discernment and faithful stewardship of God's revelations.

CONCLUSION

In prophetic ministry, confronting and overcoming fears is essential to walking authentically and powerfully in our divine calling. Recognizing these fears, not as obstacles but as opportunities for deeper reliance on God's grace, transforms our perspective and enhances our spiritual maturity. As we embrace humility, continually seek discernment, and remain open to correction, we position ourselves to be faithful stewards of God's voice. Remember, the goal of prophetic ministry is never perfection in ourselves but perfect alignment with the heart and purposes of our Heavenly Father. May each of us move forward with boldness, humility, and the assurance that God's perfect love will continually cast out all fear.

Sixteen
GOD'S LANGUAGE

SIXTEEN // GOD'S LANGUAGE

When you are in your genesis in the prophetic, whether as a prophet or a prophetic person, you quickly encounter a profound truth: God does not speak like man speaks. His voice is not merely sound; it is spirit, it is dimension, it is weight. Moreover, He communicates in a way that is entirely unique and different from how angels, who are His messengers, communicate.

In fact, angels are often sent not just to deliver messages, but to translate divine speech into a form we can grasp. A classic example is the prophet, Daniel. Though he was deeply seasoned in the ways of God, familiar with divine visions and dreams, he still struggled to fully understand what God was saying to the point that Gabriel had to be dispatched to give him clarity.

> *"Yea, whiles I was speaking in prayer, even the man Gabriel, whom I had seen in the vision at the beginning, being caused to fly swiftly, touched me about the time of the evening oblation.*
> *And he informed me, and talked with me, and said, O Daniel, I am now come forth to give thee skill and understanding.*
> *At the beginning of thy supplications the commandment came forth, and I am come to shew thee; for thou art greatly beloved: therefore understand the matter, and consider the vision."*
> Daniel 9:21-23

These scriptures always humble me. They remind me that no matter how high we ascend in the Spirit, and no matter how anointed we perceive ourselves to be, there is always more to learn. Especially in the prophetic; the higher the realm of God's communication, the more it demands from us. The greater expressions of God require a new set of skills, a sanctified vocabulary, a purified perception, and a deeper sensitivity, in order for us to hear, interpret, and respond to His voice.

There is a critical error circulating in many Christian circles regarding how God speaks, and this error has led countless people into confusion, deception, and spiritual derailment. It is this: "If I pray, God will automatically give me the interpretation of what He has said to me." This assumption is not just flawed; it is dangerous.

Many have ruined their destinies chasing what they believed to be divine direction, only to discover later they were misled, not by God, but by their own lack of spiritual skill. The problem was never that God failed to speak, but that they lacked the ability to interpret what He was saying. Let me make this clear: prayer is the portal through which God speaks, but it is not the tool that provides interpretation. Prayer opens the heavens, but understanding requires training, maturity, and often times, divine assistance.

This is why even Daniel, a beloved prophet of profound stature, did not assume that prayer alone would grant him understanding. Though God responded to his supplication immediately, Gabriel still had to be sent to give him skill and understanding.

> *"And he informed me, and talked with me, and said, O Daniel, I am now come forth to give thee skill and understanding."*
> Daniel 9:22

Receiving a word from God does not guarantee that you understand it. Even having the Holy Spirit does not automatically make you fluent in God's language. The Holy Spirit is the teacher, yes, but students must still be taught. Revelation is not microwaved; it is cultivated.

The skill of hearing God must be developed over time, through study, discipline, and humility. When we lack this skill, we must ask God to send interpreters, just as He sent Gabriel to Daniel, because the burden of interpretation does not rest on God. It rests on us, and we must be absolutely clear on this. The Bible does not simply say that Daniel and the Hebrew boys were gifted; it says God gave them skill

SIXTEEN // GOD'S LANGUAGE

in learning. That is, He granted them the divine capacity to understand, interpret, and communicate His language.

> *"As for these four children, God gave them knowledge and skill in all learning and wisdom: and Daniel had understanding in all visions and dreams."*
> Daniel 1:17

This was not just natural brilliance; it was spiritually-enabled skill. God opened up the faculties of their minds to receive His language, but it was still their responsibility to develop it. In the same way, when we become born again, God deposits the fullness of His sevenfold Spirit within us: the Spirit of the Lord, of wisdom, understanding, counsel, might, knowledge, and the fear of the Lord (Isaiah 11:2). We have the capacity to walk in divine communion, yet the question remains: how many are truly filled? How many are truly functioning in that fullness? Even the apostles, who walked with Jesus, were filled with the Holy Spirit multiple times:

- First, when the Lord Jesus breathed on them.

  > *"And when He had said this, He breathed on them, and saith unto them, Receive ye the Holy Ghost."*
  > John 20:22

- Then again, in the upper room at Pentecost:

  > *"And they were all filled with the Holy Ghost, and began to speak with other tongues, as the Spirit gave them utterance."*
  > Acts 2:4

- And again, after Peter and John were persecuted for healing the crippled man, when they gathered with the believers and were once more filled with the Holy Ghost:

"And when they had prayed, the place was shaken where they were assembled together; and they were all filled with the Holy Ghost, and they spake the word of God with boldness."
Acts 4:31

Subsequently, the question must be asked: How many of us are actually developing the capacity that God has made available to us? How many are growing in the ability to walk with Him, to speak His language, to interpret His instruction?

"Can two walk together, except they be agreed?"
Amos 3:3

And how can we agree with a God we continually fail to understand? The apostle Paul puts it plainly:

"Therefore if I know not the meaning of the voice, I shall be unto him that speaketh a barbarian, and he that speaketh shall be a barbarian unto me."
1 Corinthians 14:11

When we don't understand God's language, we become like foreigners to God, speaking past Him rather than with Him. We pray, we fast, we cry, but we remain spiritually misaligned; not for lack of zeal, but for lack of understanding.

SIXTEEN // GOD'S LANGUAGE

SHARPENING THE SKILL TO HEAR GOD

So then, the question must be asked: How do we sharpen our skills to hear God? And is hearing God the same as hearing our fellow human beings? The answer is no. Hearing God is not the same. God does not speak in fleshly tones. He speaks in spirit, and His words are often hidden in layers of symbols, impressions, scripture, and spiritual weight. To hear Him, we must grow in spiritual sensitivity, discipline, and the language of divine communication.

I used to have five dogs, and now I have four. Nesta, a golden retriever; Snoe, a Siberian husky; Ollie, an Australian shepherd; and Moko, a Rottweiler. I watch them play together, but more than that, I watch how they interact, both with each another, as well as with us, their human family. These beautiful creatures, often called man's best friend, have developed an astonishing ability to communicate. They've learned what our words mean, and they recognize our tone, our body language, and even our moods. Please hear me. They are not human, which means they don't understand our language naturally. However, through time, love, discipline, correction, and consistent exposure, they've become companions; not just through instinct, but through learned understanding. This is exactly how we must become with God.

We are spirit beings, but we are housed in flesh. Hearing God will never come from natural ability; it must be developed through intimacy, through attention, through trial and error, through stillness, and through reverence. We become better at hearing Him the more we engage with Him intentionally. Just like my dogs were trained to understand our household language, we must be trained to discern God's.

"My sheep hear my voice, and I know them, and they follow me."
John 10:27

Sheep don't recognize the shepherd's voice instantly, but they learn it. They follow because they have been led consistently.

When we hear dogs barking, to us it often sounds like noise. To them, however, it's a full-blown conversation. They are expressing emotion, sending warnings, setting boundaries, or signaling excitement. Yet many times, we silence them, not realizing they may be trying to alert us to danger. Why? Because as humans, we tend to demand to be understood, but we rarely slow down to understand others, especially those speaking a language unfamiliar to us.

This is the same posture many take toward the voice of God. We want God to make sense to us, but we do not take time to understand His language. When He speaks in ways we don't recognize, through symbols, burdens, silence, or even dreams, we silence Him, labeling it as confusion, emotion, or noise.

Consider another example. When we go to the hospital because we are unwell, the doctor does not simply treat our feeling. He or she asks questions, and then they examine symptoms. Why? Because they are trying to understand what our body is saying.

The human body is an intelligent, God-engineered creation. It has its own language, and can speak through things such as pain, fever, swelling, inflammation, weakness, discomfort, and more. Because doctors have been trained over years of study and experience, they have learned to interpret that language and accurately diagnose what's wrong, even when the patient doesn't know how to explain it.

No disease enters the body silently, and no deficiency comes without a signal. The body always gives a warning, but, if you do not understand its language, you will miss the warning, and calamity will follow. So it is with the voice of God. He speaks. He warns. He signals. But when we lack the skill and maturity to understand Him, we dismiss the sound and walk right into destruction.

We all want to hear God, but the truth is, most people don't know how to. Just as many are unaware of how their own bodies work, how their organs function, what symptoms mean, or what their soul is crying out for, many are equally ignorant of the language of the Spirit. The good news is: God has made it possible for us to mature in understanding His voice. It is not unreachable, neither is it not locked away. It is, however, spiritually discerned, and it must be developed intentionally.

> *"But the natural man receiveth not the things of the Spirit of God: for they are foolishness unto him: neither can he know them, because they are spiritually discerned."*
> 1 Corinthians 2:14

To understand how God speaks, we must first examine the means of expression God has chosen to use to communicate with human beings. Why? Because our experience is not like that of other beings. Look at angels for example. Gods speaks to them differently than He does to men. Angels do not need dreams, nor do they need parables. They behold God directly and operate in His perfect will without confusion. We on the other hand, fragile vessels of clay that we are, require symbols, metaphors, impressions, prophetic utterances, and scripture. God accommodates our humanity by wrapping eternal truth in earthly expression. This is where the journey of learning God's language truly begins: by understanding the ways He chooses to speak.

WAYS THAT GOD SPEAKS

There are so many ways that God speaks, and at least a hundred that I have personally counted. By His grace, I have been able to master about 90 percent of them. The rest I am still growing into. I have not yet become fluent in all of them, but I know that as I continue to mature, the Lord will grant me deeper understanding.

Some of the ways I first began to recognize God's voice in my prophetic journey came through the appearance of the angel who was sent to teach me, as well as through senior prophets and fathers in the faith whom I was privileged to sit under and learn from. Their instruction, combined with supernatural encounter, helped form the foundation of how I began to discern God's voice in its many expressions. For the remainder of this chapter, we will explore some of the ways that God speaks.

SCRIPTURE OR LOGOS

It is in the Scriptures that we begin to discover the nature and character of God. This discovery happens not through abstract theory, but through the lives of men and women who left behind sacred accounts of their own personal experiences with Him. In their journeys we see failures, missteps, mistakes, ignorance, and rebellion; and every time, over and over again, we also witness the unrelenting grace, mercy, and redemption of God.

This is why the Bible is not simply a book, but it is a divine conversation, preserved by the Spirit and delivered through the brokenness of man. It is through these Scriptures that God continues to speak.

> *"All scripture is given by inspiration of God, and is profitable for doctrine, for reproof, for correction, for instruction in righteousness."*
> 2 Timothy 3:16

SIXTEEN // GOD'S LANGUAGE

This is the foundation of how God speaks to us. It is by the Scriptures that we begin to recognize His voice, discern His ways, and understand the vessels He chooses. The Bible reveals not only what God said, but *how* He speaks, *why* He speaks, and *to whom* He speaks.

It is also why Scripture has the power to bring someone to salvation. That is because when you open the Bible, you are not simply reading; you are being read. You are standing in a conversation that began before you were born, and the Author is still speaking.

RHEMA OR REVELATION

> *"But He answered and said, It is written, Man shall not live by bread alone, but by every word that proceedeth out of the mouth of God."*
> Matthew 4:4

Rhema, also called revelation, is another way our precious Jesus speaks. He is not confined to a page. He is the living Word, and you can have His mouth to your ear.

This is a thriving realm, a present-tense communication of God where the Holy Spirit causes truth to leap from the invisible into your spirit. Suddenly, you know something you didn't study. You become aware of a divine reality not learned by books or logic, and it settles into your soul as though you always knew it. That is rhema. Apostle Paul explained this mystery in 1 Corinthians 2:

> *"But as it is written, Eye hath not seen, nor ear heard, neither have entered into the heart of man, the things which God hath prepared for them that love Him.*

But God hath revealed them unto us by His Spirit: for the Spirit searcheth all things, yea, the deep things of God."
1 Corinthians 2:9-10

Paul was drawing a line between the logos, which is the written Word, and the rhema, which is the revealed Word. Scripture is eternal and unchanging, but revelation is God breathing upon it and making it personal. Rhema is the moment when the Word stops being read and begins reading you.

When the Lord Jesus was tempted by Satan, He didn't engage in debate. He responded with rhema.

He quoted Deuteronomy 8:3, *"...man doth not live by bread only, but by every word that proceedeth out of the mouth of the LORD doth man live,"* but it wasn't just quoting what's written; it was God speaking directly in that moment. Then Satan, the deceiver, tried to twist Scripture. He said,

"...If thou be the Son of God, cast thyself down: for it is written, He shall give His angels charge concerning thee: and in their hands they shall bear thee up, lest at any time thou dash thy foot against a stone."
Matthew 4:6

Satan used logos because he can. Satan can handle logos. It is a manuscript. It is information. It is letters on scrolls and pages touched by human hands. He cannot, however, handle rhema, because this comes directly from the mouth of God.

Anyone can quote scripture, but not everyone can speak rhema, because rhema proceeds from the Spirit of God. You can twist verses, but you cannot twist rhema because it is not yours to manipulate. Rhema carries fire, and it carries weight; it will cut you by reason of the anointing. The Lord Jesus answered Satan with rhema and said,

SIXTEEN // GOD'S LANGUAGE

"...Thou shalt not tempt the Lord thy God."
Matthew 4:7

In other words: You know exactly who I am. I am not just a man reading the Word; I am the Word, and you are standing before your Creator. Later, the Lord Jesus recognized the voice of the Father speaking through Peter, and He also recognized the lie of the enemy speaking through Peter. The Word of God was not just something Jesus knew; it was something He was.

This is the truth: there are devils you will never defeat until you understand rhema. Rhema is not just truth, but timely truth. It is the word needed now for the season you're in. Many are searching for their identity in text alone, but who you truly are is revealed at the Master's feet, receiving, like Mary did.

"But Martha was cumbered about much serving, and came to him, and said, Lord, dost thou not care that my sister hath left me to serve alone? bid her therefore that she help me.
And Jesus answered and said unto her, Martha, Martha, thou art careful and troubled about many things:
But one thing is needful: and Mary hath chosen that good part, which shall not be taken away from her."
John 10:40-42

Rhema is not just information; rhema is visitation. It is God showing up, opening His mouth, and speaking into your soul directly, divinely, and undeniably.

STILL SMALL VOICE OR WHISPER OF THE SPIRIT

This is often described as a whisper, but it is much quieter, and far more sacred. It is not external. It is not something you hear with your ears, it is internal. Yet, it carries so much weight that it demands stillness to be perceived. This voice doesn't shout. It doesn't compete with your noise. It waits to be honored.

There was a time I was teaching a friend about how to recognize this voice. We were driving together, and I began to explain the importance of stillness and listening, not with your ears, but with your spirit. Later that day, after he dropped me off and went home, something happened.

The next morning, he was getting ready to leave the house. As he moved about, he received an impression from the Holy Spirit, saying, "Don't leave. Stay home." But it wasn't a voice like you and I hear in conversation. It was so small, so gentle, that he almost ignored it. Yet the message unsettled him. It robbed him of peace. He got into his car, still debating with that voice. Though he had never been late to work, he just couldn't shake the feeling. Moments later, he received a phone call. There had been a robbery at his workplace and people had died. He realized, that could have been him.

When he told me what happened, I asked, "How did that voice sound to you?" He said, "I can't describe it. It wasn't a thought. It wasn't audible. It was inside me, but I knew Someone had spoken. And the voice carried so much stillness, it disturbed me. I couldn't rest."

That is the still small voice.

> *"And after the earthquake a fire; but the Lord was not in the fire: and after the fire a still small voice."*
> 1 Kings 19:12

When Elijah encountered God, it was neither in the wind, nor the earthquake, nor the fire. It was in the stillness. That was how the prophet recognized the Lord, by His whisper.

> *"And thine ears shall hear a word behind thee, saying, This is the way, walk ye in it, when ye turn to the right hand, and when ye turn to the left."*
> Isaiah 30:21

This is the voice that speaks when the mind is calm, when the spirit is still, and when the heart is ready. You don't need to master every way God speaks. Start with the one He uses to reach you now, and as you grow, He will teach you more.

DARK SPEECHES (CHIYDÂH)

This is a realm of riddles, signs, parables, and prophetic codes. This is when God speaks indirectly; not because He wants to confuse you, but because He's inviting you to seek, search, and decode what He's saying. It is not casual language. It is hidden treasure.

Sometimes, the meaning behind these dark speeches lies within human understanding, but many of them require spiritual maturity to interpret. These are not surface-level messages but spirit-to-spirit codes, and often, they are only rightly understood by those seasoned in the spiritual realm.

Dark speeches is one of the ways God speaks, not just for Himself, but also through HIs messengers, such angels, ministers, and even dreams.

> *"And He said, Hear now my words: If there be a prophet among*

> *you, I the Lord will make Myself known unto him in a vision, and will speak unto him in a dream.*
> *My servant Moses is not so, who is faithful in all Mine house. With him will I speak mouth to mouth, even apparently, and not in dark speeches; and the similitude of the Lord shall he behold: wherefore then were ye not afraid to speak against My servant Moses?"*
> Numbers 12:6-8

The word used here for "dark speeches" is chîydâh; it means riddles or enigmas. God was saying: to some, I speak in riddles, but with Moses, I speak plainly. That means the dark speech is not punishment but training. God could speak plainly to all of us, and yet He doesn't, because He is processing us. He is training us to handle deeper things. He hides revelation not from us, but for us. And as we grow, we graduate.

Why doesn't God plainly say what He means? Because revelation is meant to transform, not entertain. Jeremiah and the potter's house is a perfect example (Jeremiah 18). God tells Jeremiah to go down and watch a potter work with clay. There was no explanation, only a vision, a symbol, and a process; but within it was a message: "This is what I want to do with Israel."

> *"The word which came to Jeremiah from the LORD, saying, Arise, and go down to the potter's house, and there I will cause thee to hear my words."*
> Jeremiah 18:1-2

The same took place with the prophet Isaiah. God told him to walk naked for three years, and to walk barefoot as a sign to the people.

> *"At the same time spake the LORD by Isaiah the son of Amoz,*

SIXTEEN // GOD'S LANGUAGE

saying, Go and loose the sackcloth from off thy loins, and put off thy shoe from thy foot. And he did so, walking naked and barefoot."
Isaiah 20:2

Later, God tells Ezekiel to eat dung to convey what He was speaking.

"And thou shalt eat it as barley cakes, and thou shalt bake it with dung that cometh out of man, in their sight.
And the LORD said, Even thus shall the children of Israel eat their defiled bread among the Gentiles, whither I will drive them.
Then said I, Ah Lord GOD! behold, my soul hath not been polluted: for from my youth up even till now have I not eaten of that which dieth of itself, or is torn in pieces; neither came there abominable flesh into my mouth.
Then He said unto me, Lo, I have given thee cow's dung for man's dung, and thou shalt prepare thy bread therewith."
Ezekiel 4:12-15

These were not random acts; these were dark speeches. They were riddles with prophetic meaning that seemed strange to the natural eye but were precise in heaven's language.

The Lord Jesus Himself taught this way a majority of the time. When His disciples asked why He wasn't speaking plainly to the crowd, He quoted Isaiah:

"Therefore speak I to them in parables: because they seeing see not; and hearing they hear not, neither do they understand.
And in them is fulfilled the prophecy of Esaias, which saith, By hearing ye shall hear, and shall not understand; and seeing ye shall see, and shall not perceive:

For this people's heart is waxed gross, and their ears are dull of hearing, and their eyes they have closed; lest at any time they should see with their eyes, and hear with their ears, and should understand with their heart, and should be converted, and I should heal them."
Matthew 13:13-15

Why was this? Because only those who truly seek God will go past the parable and enter the mystery. In Acts 21, the prophet Agabus comes to Paul, binds his hands and feet with a belt, and says:

"And as we tarried there many days, there came down from Judaea a certain prophet, named Agabus.
And when he was come unto us, he took Paul's girdle, and bound his own hands and feet, and said, Thus saith the Holy Ghost, So shall the Jews at Jerusalem bind the man that owneth this girdle, and shall deliver him into the hands of the Gentiles."
Acts 21:10-11

Why didn't he just say it plainly? Because that was a dark speech; it was a prophetic act carrying God's voice in symbolic form.

"Moreover the word of the Lord came unto me, saying, Jeremiah, what seest thou? And I said, I see a rod of an almond tree.
Then said the LORD unto me, Thou hast well seen: for I will hasten my word to perform it."
Jeremiah 1:11-12

God shows Jeremiah a vision and then asks him, "What do you see?" He was training him to interpret His language through what he saw. Some see clearly what God desires for them to see, while others miss it. However, that's not the issue; the issue is: God is always speaking. Many times, when God is speaking in riddles, He is waiting to see who will grow to understand.

If you want to mature in hearing God, you must be intentional. God speaks in layers, but He does not play games. Dark speeches are not for the lazy; they are for the hungry. They are for those who understand that God hides Himself in mystery so we may find Him in intimacy.

> *"It is the glory of God to conceal a thing: but the honour of kings is to search out a matter."*
> Proverbs 25:2

God is not trying to frustrate us. He wants to be discovered, and He desires to be pursued. This is why He said:

> *"And ye shall seek me, and find me, when ye shall search for me with all your heart."*
> Jeremiah 29:13

The concealed things are not punishment; they are invitations. Revelation is reserved for those who are willing to search. When God speaks in dark speeches, He is not hiding from you; He is hiding for you.

SIGNS (SÉMEION)

Signs are a beautiful and prophetic way that God speaks. The Greek word used in Scripture is *sémeion*, and it is translated as miracle, token, wonder, indication, or mark. Signs are not merely supernatural events; they are divine indicators. They point to God's will, His direction, and His movements in the earth.

From the very beginning, signs have spoken. The first message God gave to mankind wasn't spoken with His words; it was written in the stars.

> *"And God said, Let there be lights in the firmament of the heaven to divide the day from the night; and let them be for signs, and for seasons, and for days, and years."*
> Genesis 1:14

This means the heavens were not just created for beauty or timekeeping; they were prophetic instruments. The stars were God's first signs, His celestial language designed to mark moments, reveal seasons, and proclaim glory.

> *"The heavens declare the glory of God; and the firmament sheweth His handywork."*
> Psalm 19:1

It was by a sign that the birth of our Lord Jesus was revealed, through a star. The wise men, by studying that single star, discerned that a male child, a divine King, had been born. They did not need a prophetic word or an angelic visitation; they read the heavens. With the understanding of what they saw, they aligned their posture: they came to worship. They followed that star across nations and arrived at the feet of the Savior. This is the power of signs: when understood, they position you at the center of God's next move.

Mary herself was a sign. Her virginity was not just a personal detail but a supernatural token to all Israel that the Messiah had come.

> *Therefore the Lord Himself shall give you a sign; Behold, a virgin*

SIXTEEN // GOD'S LANGUAGE

shall conceive, and bear a son, and shall call his name Immanuel.
Isaiah 7:14

To this day, Mary is honored, not only for carrying Christ, but because she became a sign to the world. Her life, her purity, and her obedience marked a moment in eternity.

While He was on earth, the Lord Jesus. also used signs to speak. Referring to Jonah, He said:

For as Jonas was three days and three nights in the whale's belly; so shall the Son of man be three days and three nights in the heart of the earth.
Matthew 12:40

That was a sign. He was pointing to His own death, burial, and resurrection using the events of Jonah as a prophetic mirror. Those who had eyes to see it would have understood: He is God revealed in flesh, the Redeemer of man. We are Christians today because we believe in the sign of the resurrection, which was the ultimate sémeion. It is the wonder that validates every word He spoke, and the reason we know He is Lord.

Signs are not to be worshiped, but they are to be honored, discerned, and followed, because they point us to the God who still speaks through them. Many will miss the great return of our Lord Jesus Christ, not because He didn't speak, but because they could not discern the signs of the time. They were too busy chasing signs instead of reading them. Jesus rebuked this very thing:

"Ye hypocrites, ye can discern the face of the sky; but can ye not discern the signs of the times?"
Matthew 16:3

Even now, the signs of His coming are all around us. He is shaking the nations, awakening the earth, and stirring the Church; but just like the days of Noah, many are eating, drinking, and living unaware that the door is about to shut. And herein lies an error: men, especially the religious, always seek signs to determine whether it is God, yet that was never God's order. The message comes first. The sign is what confirms it.

> *"For the Jews require a sign, and the Greeks seek after wisdom."*
> 1 Corinthians 1:22

People have misunderstood why Jesus condemned the seeking of signs in the Gospels. They say, "But didn't Jesus give signs?" Yes, He did. However, He gave them to confirm what He had already spoken, not to convince the stubborn. Signs were never meant to replace faith; they were meant to establish it.

One of the clearest examples of this is when the Lord fed the multitude with five loaves and two fish. Thousands were fed, more than 10,000 people by some accounts. The miracle was undeniable. Then, something strange happened; the Lord Jesus left, quietly, and no one noticed. Imagine that. The Son of God left the crowd, and no one realized He was gone until they were hungry again. Their pursuit of Him wasn't out of revelation, it was out of appetite.

> *"Verily, verily, I say unto you, Ye seek me, not because ye saw the miracles, but because ye did eat of the loaves, and were filled."*
> John 6:26

When they found Him again, He corrected their motives, but they had the audacity to ask Him for another sign.

> *"They said therefore unto Him, What sign shewest Thou then,*

SIXTEEN // GOD'S LANGUAGE

that we may see, and believe Thee? what dost Thou work?"
John 6:30

The Lord was grieved. He had fed them, healed them, and walked among them, yet they still missed Him. They were seeking the stamp, not the scroll. They were chasing miracles, but ignoring the message. The Lord was telling them: You missed Me. I was here, and you missed Me.

Signs are not the substance; they are the seal. The miracle was never the meal; it was the Messenger. Hear this clearly: if you are seeking the stamp, you will miss the message. If you are waiting for a wonder before you believe, your heart has already wandered.

Though signs confirm what God is saying, they are not what God is saying. They are the echo, not the voice. Signs are external, and because they are external, they can be infiltrated by the enemy. Those who chase after signs without understanding are often the first to fall into deception. This is why the Bible warns us:

"For there shall arise false Christs, and false prophets, and shall shew great signs and wonders; insomuch that, if it were possible, they shall deceive the very elect."
Matthew 24:24

These deceivers offer a stamp without a message, power without truth, and wonders without the Word. I have seen this in my own ministry. There were people whom God used me to heal, some that were delivered from barrenness, and others that were set free from demonic bondage; yet, after receiving their miracle, they left the church. I went before the Lord and asked, *"Why, after such wonders among them?"* And He answered me: *"They wanted the miracle without the message. They left Me, not you."*

"They went out from us, but they were not of us; for if they had been of us, they would no doubt have continued with us: but they went out, that they might be made manifest that they were not all of us."
1 John 2:19

In that moment, I understood: it wasn't personal, it was prophetic. This is why, even though Jesus Christ our God performed undeniable signs and miracles, many till did not believe.

"But though He had done so many miracles before them, yet they believed not on Him."
John 12:37

They were chasing signs, not truth. They sought the gift, but not the Giver. They wanted the benefit, but not the voice. And when pressure came and the accusers rose, the same crowd that shouted:

"…Hosanna to the Son of David: Blessed is He that cometh in the name of the Lord; Hosanna in the highest!"
Matthew 21:9

within 48 hours cried out:

"…Crucify Him!"
Matthew 27:22 NIV

Why? Because they never wanted the Message. They only wanted the miracle.

SIXTEEN // GOD'S LANGUAGE

OPEN VISIONS

I personally believe that vision is God's primary language. From the very beginning of Scripture, we see that God is a visual God. His process is always one of seeing, then forming, and then declaring. This is why open vision is not just one of the ways God speaks; it may be the most foundational.

In Genesis chapter 2 we read:

"And God blessed the seventh day, and sanctified it: because that in it He had rested from all His work which God created and made."
Genesis 2:3

This verse reveals something deeper when you look closely. The word "created" speaks of conception, meaning, what was formed in the mind of God. The word "made" speaks of manifestation, meaning, what was constructed and assembled. Creation begins in vision. God saw it before He spoke it. He formed it in Himself before He manifested it in the world. Genesis 1 gives us this powerful insight:

"And God saw every thing that He had made, and, behold, it was very good. And the evening and the morning were the sixth day."
Genesis 1:31

Even God Himself looked at what He had envisioned and made. He saw it. He is not just a speaking God. He is a seeing God. And because we are made in His image, God will often speak to us by allowing us to see what He is saying before we understand it, or even before it manifests.

This is what open vision is: God pulling back the veil and letting you behold what is already known in heaven. You don't dream it nor do you imagine it; it stands in front of you in real time. In that moment, you are no longer just hearing from God; you are beholding Him.

This is why there is a distinction between a Seer and a Prophet. A Prophet is moved by the Spirit. He hears and speaks what he has not seen; the Spirit of the Lord rests upon him and places the Word of the Lord in his mouth. A Seer (a "Chozeh" in Hebrew) sees the mind of God. He doesn't just hear it, he beholds it. He operates by divine sight and he speaks from what he has seen, not just what he has sensed.

> *"Beforetime in Israel, when a man went to inquire of God, thus he spake, Come, and let us go to the seer: for he that is now called a Prophet was beforetime called a Seer."*
> 1 Samuel 9:9

This experience is not just for prophets, it is for every believer. God desires to reveal Himself in this way to anyone who is willing, clean, and available.

Often, God uses open visions to convict even those who are far from Him in order to bring them into divine encounter. Consider Saul on the road to Damascus: He saw a light brighter than the sun and heard the voice of Jesus.

> *"And he fell to the earth, and heard a voice saying unto him, Saul, Saul, why persecutest thou Me?"*
> Acts 9:4

Everyone around him heard something, but only Saul saw the Lord. And though he did not yet know Jesus by name, the encounter was so overwhelming that he cried,

> *"Who art thou, Lord?..."*
> Acts 9:5

SIXTEEN // GOD'S LANGUAGE

He *knew* by the magnitude of that vision that he was standing before the Lord. This is the power of an open vision. You don't interpret it, you actively encounter it. There is no need for decoding, because God Himself is revealing His form, His voice, or His realm directly to you.

Ezekiel experienced this by the river Chebar:

"Now it came to pass in the thirtieth year, in the fourth month, in the fifth day of the month, as I was among the captives by the river of Chebar, that the heavens were opened, and I saw visions of God."
Ezekiel 1:1

He saw the four living creatures, wheels within wheels, and the throne of God. It wasn't imagination, and it wasn't a dream. That was a visitation. Open visions bypass your senses and speak to your spirit. They are a high language of God that is pure, direct, and unmistakable. When God wants to mark you forever, He may allow you to see. And once you have seen, you cannot unsee.

Walking in this realm of open visions is not casual. It is a dimension reserved for those God chooses, and for those who have been spiritually developed and consecrated through deep intimacy, purity, and submission. In later books we will discuss how to enter fully into this realm, and we will explore the protocols, pathways, and postures required to live in continual vision. For now, know this: this realm is real, and it is attainable by those who are willing to become what the vision requires.

CLOSED VISIONS

This is an experience unlike an open vision, where those around you may feel the presence of God, hear a sound, or sense something supernatural, yet not understand the meaning. A closed vision takes place within your inner man, or in other words, your spirit.

As I just shared, a good example of an open vision is found in the life of Paul on his way to persecute Christians. He had a direct encounter with the Lord Jesus, and it affected everyone around him. They saw a light and heard a sound, but did not understand the voice. That was an open vision that spilled over into the physical realm.

A closed vision is different in that you do not lose awareness of your surroundings. While you remain alert and conscious, your spirit is watching something heaven is showing you, and those around you have no idea it's happening.

This is the most common way God speaks to me during services. He will open my spiritual eyes and show me things. I will see visions, prophetic pictures, angelic activity, and receive insight and foresight, all within my spirit. To everyone else, I look completely normal, but within me, a vision is unfolding.

Open visions have happened to me during services too, though they are rare. When they do occur, they are undeniably noticeable. The atmosphere changes and the weight of God's presence becomes tangible. People can feel something is happening. With closed visions, the encounter is personal and private, though just as powerful. God speaks directly to your spirit without disrupting your external environment.

Closed visions train your spirit to become sensitive. They teach you how to see without spectacle, and to hear without distraction. A perfect example of a closed vision is found in Luke chapter 5, where Jesus is teaching a multitude. In the middle of His message, He discerns their internal dialogue.

SIXTEEN // GOD'S LANGUAGE

"But when Jesus perceived their thoughts, He answering said unto them, What reason ye in your hearts?"
Luke 5:22

How did He do that? To properly understand this, we must fully grasp that Jesus Christ was a hundred percent human while He lived on earth. If He had any divine advantage in His earthly life, His sacrifice would not be complete. He came as fully man, representing all our weaknesses, limitations, and temptations, and yet He was without sin. This moment in the gospels wasn't the Lord Jesus operating with divine omniscience; rather, it was Him walking in the fullness of the Spirit and demonstrating what a human being can perceive when in tune with God.

To understand this, we must first understand how thoughts work.

- Active imagination is when we intentionally search our subconscious and build images with intent.
- Passive thoughts are spontaneous and often uninvited; they are casual, and usually triggered by memories, emotions, or surroundings.

Either way, thoughts are neither random nor static. They are made up of images, and in the spirit realm those images speak. That is why Jesus *saw* their thoughts. To the carnal mind, thoughts are silent; but in the spirit, thoughts have form, shape, and meaning. They are visual expressions. In that moment, the Lord Jesus saw that although each person formed their thoughts individually, in the spirit they all were saying the same thing.

"And immediately when Jesus perceived in His spirit that they so

reasoned within themselves, He said unto them, Why reason ye these things in your hearts?"
Mark 2:8

"But Jesus did not commit Himself unto them, because He knew all men,
And needed not that any should testify of man: for He knew what was in man."
John 2:24-25

These are all examples of closed visions in operation. The Lord Jesus was seeing in His spirit what others were processing in their souls. By the mercies and grace of God, I have experienced this many times. I can be speaking to someone, and at the same time, the Holy Spirit will begin to show me things, even the intentions of their thoughts, through vision. This doesn't mean I read minds. It means the Spirit translates the spiritual activity around a person and reveals it visually; because, as I said before, God's primary language is visual.

DREAMS

"And He said, Hear now my words: If there be a prophet among you, I the LORD will make myself known unto him in a vision, and will speak unto him in a dream."
Numbers 12:6

Dreams are one of the languages of God, and according to Numbers 12:6, they are a legitimate expression of His voice. This means that anyone who dreams is already, in one way or another,

SIXTEEN // GOD'S LANGUAGE

touching the realm where God speaks.

Now, this does not mean that every dream is from God. Some dreams are born of the soul, in that they are manifestations of what you have consumed emotionally, mentally, or spiritually throughout the day or even at past points in your life. However, when God speaks through a dream, it is never empty. It is layered, weighty, and strategic. This is because dreams require interpretation.

> *"And they said unto him, We have dreamed a dream, and there is no interpreter of it. And Joseph said unto them, Do not interpretations belong to God? tell me them, I pray you."*
> Genesis 40:8

In this moment, Joseph stood in the place of spiritual intelligence; not only because he could dream, but because he understood what dreams meant.

Dreamers are many, but interpreters are rare. Those who can interpret God's language in the night season become solution-carriers. Joseph, as his story unfolded, was much more than just an interpreter of dreams; he shifted nations because he could understand what God was saying in a hidden form. In Genesis chapter 41, Pharaoh had a dream that no one in all of Egypt could interpret. Joseph was called upon, and because of his relationship with God, he unlocked the mystery, and by that one interpretation an entire kingdom was preserved and Israel was secured within it.

Dreams are not entertainment. They are encrypted messages, prophecies wrapped in mystery. I will go much deeper into this in a book soon to come, called *"The Dreaming Prophets' Manual."* Therein I will teach on the different types of dreams, the laws of interpretation, the role of angelic visitations, soul pollution, spiritual decoding, and how to discern God's voice from your own inner noise.

In the meantime, understand this: if God is speaking in your sleep, it means you matter to Him. The question is, do you have the wisdom to interpret what He's saying?

> *"For God speaketh once, yea twice, yet man perceiveth it not.*
> *In a dream, in a vision of the night, when deep sleep falleth upon men, in slumberings upon the bed;*
> *Then He openeth the ears of men, and sealeth their instruction."*
> Job 33:14-16

This passage is both encouraging and corrective. It comforts us with the truth that God is deeply interested in our sleep, finding an opportunity to speak to us in that stillness. At the same time, it confronts us with the reality that He does speak to us, but we often do not perceive it. What this means is that when we lay our heads down every night, heaven may be attempting to start a conversation with us; but if we are not discerning, we will sleep through instruction. We will miss the scroll because we never expected a voice. Statistically, human beings spend one-third of their lives sleeping. So if, for example, one was to live to be seventy-five years old, they would have spent approximately 9,490 days asleep, which is about twenty-five years in total. Just imagine what God could do with twenty-five years of uninterrupted access to your spirit!

If you truly understand the realm of dreams, you will realize you are not missing out on life when you sleep, because you are actually entering the classroom of the Spirit. The tragedy is that for many, sleep is only either physical rest or emotional escape from the pressures of life. Thankfully, for those who walk with God, sleep is an altar, and dreaming becomes a chance to touch the hem of the garment of our Master Jesus.

Every dream from God lives in you. So, here is my charge to you: pray, and ask God to bring His voice back. Ask Him to resurrect the word He gave you in the night, that you may fulfill His will in the

SIXTEEN // GOD'S LANGUAGE

day.

VISIONS OF THE NIGHT

This is the highest realm of dreams. It is a dimension where the boundary between the spirit and the natural becomes so thin, that you awaken feeling as though what you were dreaming truly happened. A vision of the night is not like ordinary dreaming. In this realm, a world is unlocked; one that is so vivid and so real, that when you come out of it, it leaves an imprint on your soul.

One of the clearest examples of this is Joseph, the earthly father of Jesus. The angel Gabriel appeared to him in a vision of the night, telling him that Mary was pregnant with the Savior of the world, and that what she carried was not scandal, but God incarnate.

> *"But while he thought on these things, behold, the angel of the Lord appeared unto him in a dream, saying, Joseph, thou son of David, fear not to take unto thee Mary thy wife: for that which is conceived in her is of the Holy Ghost."*
> Matthew 1:20

What is remarkable is this: Joseph never doubted it. He didn't wrestle with it, nor question whether it was his own thoughts. How was this possible? It is because visions of the night carry a supernatural clarity. The voice is so distinct, and the presence so real, that your spirit knows it is not imagination. Joseph knew that it was a divine encounter.

He would go on to receive other visions of the night, such as the one where he was told to flee to Egypt with Mary and the child, and again when he was told it was safe to return.

> *"And when they were departed, behold, the angel of the Lord appeareth to Joseph in a dream, saying, Arise, and take the young child and His mother, and flee into Egypt, and be thou there until I bring thee word: for Herod will seek the young child to destroy Him."*
> Matthew 2:13

> *"But when Herod was dead, behold, an angel of the Lord appeareth in a dream to Joseph in Egypt,*
> *Saying, Arise, and take the young child and His mother, and go into the land of Israel: for they are dead which sought the young child's life."*
> Matthew 2:19-20

He was led not by audible voices in the day, but by visions in the night. And because he obeyed, the life of Jesus was preserved.

The prophet Daniel also experienced this realm. Gabriel appeared to him in visions and dreams with messages that shook kingdoms and unveiled timelines.

> *"And whiles I was speaking, and praying, and confessing my sin and the sin of my people Israel, and presenting my supplication before the LORD my God for the holy mountain of my God;*
> *Yea, whiles I was speaking in prayer, even the man Gabriel, whom I had seen in the vision at the beginning, being caused to fly swiftly, touched me about the time of the evening oblation.*
> *And he informed me, and talked with me, and said, O Daniel, I am now come forth to give thee skill and understanding."*
> Daniel 9:20-22

These visions required no interpretation because they were direct transmissions from heaven. When God speaks in this realm, your spirit receives it as instruction, not suggestion. This did not begin with Joseph or Daniel; it actually began in the garden, in Genesis.

Adam was the first man to explore the realm of the vision of the night. God put him into a deep sleep, not to rest him, but to reveal something eternal.

> *"And the LORD God caused a deep sleep to fall upon Adam, and he slept: and he took one of his ribs, and closed up the flesh instead thereof;*
> *And the rib, which the LORD God had taken from man, made He a woman, and brought her unto the man."*
> Genesis 2:21-22

When Adam awoke and Eve was brought to him, he didn't just see her, he recognized her.

> *"And Adam said, This is now bone of my bones, and flesh of my flesh: she shall be called Woman, because she was taken out of Man."*
> Genesis 2:23

How did he know this? He knew it because in that deep sleep, he saw the creation of man in Genesis chapter 1 come to life.

> *"And God said, Let us make man in Our image, after our likeness: and let them have dominion over the fish of the sea, and over the fowl of the air, and over the cattle, and over all the earth, and over every creeping thing that creepeth upon the earth.*
> *So God created man in His own image, in the image of God*
>
> *created He him; male and female created He them."*
> Genesis 1:26-27

He watched the vision of God creating male and female play out before him, and when he awoke, he knew her assignment, her origin, and her name.

This is the power of the vision of the night. It marks you with understanding, and awakens memory in your spirit of things your mind has never learned. It does not ask you to believe, but rather, it causes you to know.

TRANCES (EKSTASIS)

The experience called trance, *ekstasis* in Greek, literally means "to be out of oneself." It is a supernatural state in which your natural awareness is suspended, and your spirit becomes fully immersed in the realm of God. This is a divine channel that God has used from the beginning to speak to His people. It is not new, nor is it mystical. It is biblical.

> *"On the morrow, as they went on their journey, and drew nigh unto the city, Peter went up upon the housetop to pray about the sixth hour:*
> *And he became very hungry, and would have eaten: but while they made ready, he fell into a trance [ekstasis]."*
> Acts 10:9-10

In the trance, Peter received a vision that would change Church history forever, as God revealed that the Gospel was not just for the Jews but for the Gentiles also. One supernatural moment of ekstasis carried a revelation that centuries of religion could not produce. Unfortunately, just like many sacred things, this too has been abused

SIXTEEN // GOD'S LANGUAGE

by darkness.

Always remember, the devil cannot create. He can only corrupt because he has no power to invent. His only agenda is to pervert what God designed, using it to deceive, to distract, and to detour humanity from Yahweh, our precious Creator.

Think of the spiritual world like this: Roads were created to connect cities, to facilitate movement, and to help in times of emergency. However, once those roads are built, anyone can use them. An ambulance can now reach its destination faster because of the road; and so can a thief. The devil did not build the road, God did; but Satan will use the same structure God made to invade, confuse, and imitate divine communication.

Such is the case with trances. God created this realm for encounter, revelation, and instruction. Angels use these pathways to appear, and the Holy Spirit uses them to download visions and prophetic insight. But demonic spirits, because they are illegal, try to hijack what God ordained in order to trap people with deception, especially those who are spiritually untrained.

This is why we must be anchored in truth and Scripture. The trance state is real, and it is sacred. Therefore, it must be entered by those who walk in light, not those who chase power.

> *"And he became very hungry, and would have eaten: but while they made ready, he fell into a trance,*
> *And saw heaven opened, and a certain vessel descending unto him, as it had been a great sheet knit at the four corners, and let down to the earth."*
> Acts 10:10-11

Peter wasn't conjuring a spirit, nor was he performing. He was praying, and in that holy place, heaven opened.

I repeat: trances are not demonic, they are biblical. However, they must be discerned, guarded, and understood, so that what God designed as a highway of glory does not become, through ignorance, a pathway to confusion.

The reason I am bringing this to your attention is because the trance state can be entered into in many different ways, but only one way is righteous, and that is through the Spirit of God, in alignment with His Word and nature.

In today's world, so many are seeking for enlightenment, but they are seeking without light. As a result, they are trapping themselves in spiritual entanglements that will take great mercy and deep deliverance to escape, all because of their pursuit.

Entering a trance is not difficult. It doesn't require holiness; it only demands access. When people are looking only for an experience to validate their personal truth, they become vulnerable to the one who is the father of lies.

Let me be very clear: There is only one Truth, and His name is Jesus Christ.

> *"Jesus saith unto him, I am the way, the truth, and the life: no man cometh unto the Father, but by Me."*
> John 14:6

There was a young man I once prayed for who believed he was being led by the Holy Spirit. He wanted to see God so badly, and he wanted to be used of God. The devil took advantage of his foolish zeal, because is looking for an encounter in every way possible. Satan deceived him and told him that he was the greatest prophet to ever live; that God would do with him that which He had done with Peter in scripture. He further led him to believe the things he would do had never been seen before, because he was the reincarnation of the great Prophet Elijah. The young man believed the lies, and was convinced that he was one of the last two witnesses before the coming of the

SIXTEEN // GOD'S LANGUAGE

Lord.

The voice of the deceiver then instructed him to go to a bus station near his home; there, he would find a crippled man and he should pray for him. The man would be healed, because he had the power to set him free, and as a result, his fame will spread and everyone would know him. Lo and behold, things unfolded just as the voice told him. When the young man prayed for the crippled man at that bus station, the man did not get healed, but he instantly became crippled. When his mother brought him to church to be prayed for, he still believed it was God speaking to him.

This is why I am very cautious of young ministers who come to me but their motivation is fame. That is not the Spirit of God. Satan will never exalt the Lord; he will exalt you, because he knows that the deepest desire of man is to be exalted. This is how he traps many.

> *"And no marvel; for Satan himself is transformed into an angel of light."*
> 2 Corinthians 11:14

After I prayed for the young man and he was instantly healed, that is when he realized that he had been driven by his own zeal, and was doing what God had not sent him to do. This is just one example out of the countless cases where the Lord has used me to help people who had fallen into the deception of the enemy because of their desire to have a spiritual encounter. These encounters are not awakening. They are spiritual invasions, and they are not harmless.

The trance state is not a neutral state. You must ask: Who invited me? Who is guiding me? Who is speaking? Only in the presence of the Lord Jesus, in prayer, consecration, and truth, can the trance realm be entered safely and righteously.

Scripture gives us many beautiful examples of men who were summoned by God into His presence.

> *"And it came to pass, that, when I was come again to Jerusalem, even while I prayed in the temple, I was in a trance;*
> *And saw Him saying unto me, Make haste, and get thee quickly out of Jerusalem: for they will not receive thy testimony concerning Me."*
> Acts 22:17-18

Paul wasn't seeking an experience. He was seeking God, and God met him.

So, then, the question becomes: how do I experience this realm while protecting myself from Satan's infiltration? It begins with the posture of your heart. When your heart is set on God with right and pure motives, you are already safe. The Lord has made us a promise:

> *"Thou wilt keep him in perfect peace, whose mind is stayed on Thee: because he trusteth in Thee."*
> Isaiah 26:3

We mustn't chase experiences, nor should we pursue encounters, for the sake of spiritual thrills. We are to seek the Master, our Savior. Should He choose to speak, visit, or reveal Himself to us, we are to receive it with gratitude and reverence.

> *"In all thy ways acknowledge Him, and He shall direct thy paths."*
> Proverbs 3:6

When you make Jesus Christ the pursuit, every trance becomes safe, every vision is aligned, and every experience is sanctified; because it is not about what you see, but about the One who sends it.

Here are four biblical ways that God can use to bring you into a holy trance:

SIXTEEN // GOD'S LANGUAGE

1. PRAYER

When you enter into deep, sincere prayer, with full concentration, full surrender, and undistracted longing, you may be drawn into ekstasis, where your natural senses are suspended, and your spirit is caught up.

"Peter went up upon the housetop to pray... he fell into a trance."
Acts 10:9-10

Trance has to do with engagement, not emotion. When you pray from the depths of your spirit, heaven opens.

2. MEDITATION OF THE WORD

The Word of God is alive. When you meditate deeply, turning Scripture over and over in your heart, it can unlock divine trance states where revelation pours in.

"But his delight is in the law of the Lord; and in His law doth he meditate day and night."
Psalm 1:2

Meditation is not emptiness; it is fullness focused on Him. When your spirit is saturated in the Word, God may lift you into revelatory stillness, where His Spirit unveils mysteries you could not perceive in the natural.

3. INTENSE PRAISE AND WORSHIP

When praise and worship flow from the depths of your being pure, holy, and free of performance, it can usher you into a realm where time disappears and God's presence overshadows you. In those moments, the Spirit of God may arrest your senses and take you into ekstasis, where your body is still, but your spirit is fully awake.

"It came even to pass, as the trumpeters and singers were as one, to make one sound to be heard in praising and thanking the LORD; and when they lifted up their voice with the trumpets and cymbals and instruments of musick, and praised the LORD, saying, For He is good; for His mercy endureth for ever: that then the house was filled with a cloud, even the house of the LORD; So that the priests could not stand to minister by reason of the cloud: for the glory of the LORD had filled the house of God."
2 Chronicles 5:13-14

4. FASTING

Fasting is not just abstaining from food; it is the consecration of your appetite, attention, and desires to God. When done in purity and alignment with the Holy Spirit, fasting weakens the flesh and sharpens the spirit. This state of surrender often creates a spiritual sensitivity that opens you to deeper realms of God's communication, including ekstasis.

In your pursuit to hear the voice of God, protect your pursuit by fixing your heart on the Lord Jesus. Let Him be your reason, and let Truth be your anchor. Should He choose to draw you into trance, vision, or encounter, receive it with holy fear, thanksgiving, and readiness to obey. Purity protects, obedience preserves, and Christ alone is the gate.

SIXTEEN // GOD'S LANGUAGE

OUTER BODY EXPERIENCES

An outer body experience, when initiated by God, is a holy encounter where your consciousness, which is your spirit, is pulled out of the natural realm and taken into the unseen world. This realm is completely different from lucid dreaming or astral projection, as it is not something man can fabricate or force. Only God can call up the spirit of man.

As I mentioned previously regarding trances, this is another realm that has been perverted by those practicing dark arts. The occult has long used altered states and rituals to induce spiritual experiences, but many of them don't realize that they are not rising into light. They are being lured by devils trying to escape the lower realms of the underworld, reaching up to entangle human souls. What they call enlightenment is actually entrapment. Again: the enemy cannot create. He can only counterfeit.

When God initiates an outer body experience, and when He lifts your spirit beyond the flesh, it is not confusing, chaotic, or demonic. It is divine. Throughout Scripture, we see men and women whom God called out of their bodies, and each time, they were shocked by what they encountered. The veil was torn as they were caught up, and their entire perspective shifted.

> *"It is not expedient for me doubtless to glory. I will come to visions and revelations of the Lord.*
> *I knew a man in Christ above fourteen years ago, (whether in the body, I cannot tell; or whether out of the body, I cannot tell: God knoweth;) such an one caught up to the third heaven."*
> 2 Corinthians 12:1-2

Paul was describing something so sacred he had no words for it. He didn't know if he was in his body or out of it; all he knew was that he was caught up.

This experience is the highest form of spiritual communication, because your spirit has left its earthly vessel and entered a heavenly domain. When we receive visions, dreams, trances, signs, or closed visions, all those are shadows; outer body experiences are the substance. They are glimpses of what the believer will permanently step into once they leave this physical life.

> *"For to me to live is Christ, and to die is gain."*
> Philippians 1:21

Only a man who has seen the other side would speak in this manner about leaving this world.

> *"For we know that if our earthly house of this tabernacle were dissolved, we have a building of God, an house not made with hands, eternal in the heavens."*
> 2 Corinthians 5:1

This is why Paul longed to go. He had seen it.

At the core, God does not speak to your body; and He does not even speak to your soul first. God speaks to your spirit, and through it, revelation is pushed into the soul, where it becomes understanding. This body is simply our earthly tent, and the truth is, it is a limitation. There is a world beyond it, which God desires to reveal to His people. At times, with great mercy and purpose, He may lift you out to show you who He is, what is to come, or who you really are in Him. But again, remember this: no man can initiate this realm rightly; it *must* be God. Anything else is imitation, and imitation opens doors to deception. When it is God, you'll know, because the experience will bring holy fear, overwhelming love, eternal clarity, and deeper humility.

SIXTEEN // GOD'S LANGUAGE

And when you return to your body, you will never be the same again.

There are things that are virtually impossible to attain while still in this body. When God summons your spirit and calls you out of your flesh and brings you into His presence, you begin to realize just how much we are restricted by this earthly vessel. Once you've encountered the heavenly realm, it becomes difficult to express it to those who've never left the natural. You may try to explain it, but words fail to accurately convey it; this is because language belongs to the earth, whereas what you saw belongs to eternity. This is why the Lord Jesus said to Nicodemus:

> *"If I have told you earthly things, and ye believe not, how shall ye believe, if I tell you of heavenly things?"*
> John 3:12

He also said to His disciples:

> *"I have yet many things to say unto you, but ye cannot bear them now."*
> John 16:12

The Master was not withholding those things out of secrecy; rather, He was shielding them from overload. Their capacity hadn't yet caught up with His revelation.

In the spirit, your capacity explodes. When you are outside of your body, and your spirit stands before God, your comprehension, intelligence, discernment, and absorption are all heightened. You finally begin to understand what it means to be a new creature in Christ; not because of theology, but because of encounter. This is a realm where there is no confusion, no inner conflict, and no fog. You enter a state where the Lord can impart what feels like 10 million years of revelation in a microsecond, and your spirit will absorb it like a sponge.

The moment you're outside of your body, you realize: Truth is not learned, it is revealed. When you return to the natural, you carry a portion of eternity inside of time.

Here are some beautiful examples of men who were summoned by God into His presence:

EZEKIEL: THE PROPHET OF DIVINE TRANSPORT

Ezekiel is one of the clearest examples of a man who was repeatedly taken by the Spirit of God. His encounters were vivid, physical, and spiritual, marking him forever.

"Then the Spirit took me up, and I heard behind me a voice of a great rushing, saying, Blessed be the glory of the LORD from His place."
Ezekiel 3:12

"So the spirit lifted me up, and took me away, and I went in bitterness, in the heat of my spirit; but the hand of the LORD was strong upon me."
Ezekiel 3:14

"The hand of the LORD was upon me, and carried me out in the Spirit of the LORD, and set me down in the midst of the valley which was full of bones."
Ezekiel 37:1

JOHN THE APOSTLE: CARRIED INTO HEAVENLY REALMS

John was on the island of Patmos, exiled for the testimony of

SIXTEEN // GOD'S LANGUAGE

Jesus Christ. While isolated on earth, he was summoned into heaven.

"I was in the Spirit on the Lord's day, and heard behind me a great voice, as of a trumpet."
Revelation 1:10

"And immediately I was in the spirit: and, behold, a throne was set in heaven, and One sat on the throne."
Revelation 4:2

This was not Apostle John's imagination; he was in fact present in the heavenly dimension.

ELIJAH: THE MASTER PROPHET

Elijah was so frequently moved by the Spirit that even kings and messengers feared approaching him, knowing God could take him at any moment.

"And it shall come to pass, as soon as I am gone from thee, that the Spirit of the LORD shall carry thee whither I know not; and so when I come and tell Ahab, and he cannot find thee, he shall slay me: but I thy servant fear the LORD from my youth."
1 Kings 18:12

Elijah lived in such a level of divine transport that men hesitated to leave his presence for fear that God would take him elsewhere. This was the reason why Elisha refused to leave his side when he was to be taken up to heaven. He was like the wind.

"The wind bloweth where it listeth, and thou hearest the sound thereof, but canst not tell whence it cometh, and whither it goeth: so is every one that is born of the Spirit."
John 3:8

MOSES: SUMMONED INTO THE CLOUD OF GLORY

When Moses was called into the thick cloud of God's presence on Mount Sinai, he was taken up into divine dimensions. It was there he received the blueprints of creation and eternity.

"And Moses went up into the mount, and a cloud covered the mount.
And the glory of the LORD abode upon mount Sinai, and the cloud covered it six days: and the seventh day He called unto Moses out of the midst of the cloud."
Exodus 24:15-16

It was through such encounters that Moses was able to write the first five books of the Bible, and according to ancient tradition, even the account of creation itself.

I want you to remember this: God desires to build each of us up by speaking to us. It is His desire that we would yearn to see Him and hear from Him, but never at the expense of reverence or foundation. Do not lift experience above God, and do not let your visions, trances, or encounters become your doctrine. Faith does not come by experience; it comes by His Word. Let every encounter confirm the Word.

"So then faith cometh by hearing, and hearing by the word of

SIXTEEN // GOD'S LANGUAGE

God."
Romans 10:17

Let every vision lead you back to Scripture, and let every revelation make you more like the Lord Jesus. Seek Him and not signs. Desire Him, not dimensions. Above all, be rooted in truth.

Conclusion
HE THAT HATH AN EAR

"He that hath an ear, let him hear what the Spirit saith unto the churches."
Revelation 2:7

From the beginning of this book, we have journeyed through the many ways God speaks. We've explored Scripture, both the logos and the rhema, dreams, visions, trances, symbols, signs, and even the still small voice within. We've touched dimensions of the spirit that are holy, weighty, and not to be mishandled.

Now, as we come to the end, I say this to you: do not seek the sound, seek the Speaker. If you forget everything else, remember this: **God's voice is not entertainment. It is encounter.** It is not given to satisfy curiosity, but to cultivate intimacy. It is not meant to excite but to transform.

A RECAP OF THE VOICE OF GOD

God speaks in many ways, but His voice is always rooted in **truth**, confirmed by **His Word**, and filled with **purpose**:

- **Scripture** is the foundation; it is the written voice of God.
- **Rhema** is the breathed word, fresh revelation that unlocks hidden doors.
- **The still small voice** is God's whisper to your spirit, gentle but undeniable.
- **Dreams and visions** are divine communication through symbolic or visual expression.
- **Trances and outer body experiences** are holy dimensions, entered only by God's summons.
- **Closed and open visions**, signs, and thoughts all are languages of

the Spirit.

You must also remember this: the enemy can imitate form but not presence. He can create noise, but not the weight of glory. Many are deceived today because they seek the experience more than they seek the Lord.

SEEK THE LORD, NOT THE MANIFESTATION

We live in a generation obsessed with spiritual sensation. Understand that seeking spiritual encounters without the Word, without submission, and without purity is not maturity; it is rebellion dressed in hunger.
You do not prove your closeness to God by the frequency of your visions. You prove it by your obedience, your humility, and your transformation. God is not impressed with your ability to hear Him. He is pleased when what you hear shapes who you are.

> *"And be ye doers of the word, and not hearers only, deceiving your own selves."*
> James 1:22

PURITY IS THE PREREQUISITE

Without holiness, no man shall see the Lord; not in this life, nor in the next. God may allow immature ears to hear in seasons of mercy, but sustained communication requires purity. If your soul is filled with bitterness, unforgiveness, addiction, pride, and distraction, you will mistake your own voice or even demonic influence for His.

Purity is not perfection, it is posture. It is a heart that says:

"Search me, O God, and know my heart: try me, and know my thoughts."
Psalm 139:23

"Create in me a clean heart, O God; and renew a right spirit within me."
Psalm 51:10

Only a renewed mind can discern the voice of a holy God.

Let this be your pursuit and never ending prayer: *"Lord, I don't want more experiences. I want more of You."* When you have Him, the rest will come. Visions will come, dreams will come, and revelation will come. Even more importantly, obedience, brokenness, and holiness will come. That is what God is after.

A FINAL CHARGE

You now know that God speaks. He speaks in many ways, to many people, and for many purposes. The ones who truly hear are not the most gifted; they are the most surrendered. And so I end this book with the words the Lord Jesus spoke to every church in Revelation:

"He that hath an ear, let him hear what the Spirit saith…"

CONCLUSION: HE THAT HATH AN EAR

Not what the flesh desires, not what the world affirms, nor what your fear suggests. Only what the Spirit saith. May you be one who hears, and lives.

Final Prayer

Father, I pray for the man and woman of God reading this book, this book that is filled with Your truth, wisdom, and knowledge.

Father, keep them for Your own name's sake, and show them mercy as they continually search for You. Give them the grace to find You, and show them mighty things which they do not know, just as Your Word declares.

Father, silence the enemy for them as they grow in the awareness of Your voice, and by Your Spirit, secure them by showing them their hearts always, so that they may remain humble and far from pride.

Reveal Your only Son Jesus to them continually, that they may know You. And above all, Father, glorify Yourself through them.

In Jesus' mighty name, Amen.

For more teachings by Dr. Lovy L. Elias, visit www.prophetlovy.com.

www.ingramcontent.com/pod-product-compliance
Lightning Source LLC
Chambersburg PA
CBHW030110240426
43661CB00031B/1364/J